D1721753

The No-Code Startup: Quickly Build and Validate Startup Ideas

Written by Daniel Carr
Published by Cornell-David Publishing House

Index

1. Introduction: The Power of No-Code MVPs

1.1 Embracing the No-Code Revolution for Rapid MVP Development

The world of entrepreneurship has evolved dramatically over the last few years, with the digital era providing us with a wide range of tools and resources to bring our ideas to life faster and more efficiently than ever before. Enter the realm of no-code tools – a new wave of software applications that allows non-technical people, such as entrepreneurs and designers, to bring their startup ideas to fruition without having to rely on traditional software development.

But what exactly makes no-code MVPs (Minimum Viable Products) so powerful, and how can they help today's budding entrepreneurs to validate their ideas quickly and move toward product-market fit? In this section, we'll be exploring the benefits of no-code platforms, the basic principles behind MVPs, and how the combination of the two can propel your startup idea to the next level.

1.1.1 Breaking Down the Barriers to Entry

One of the most significant hurdles growing startups often face is the pressure to hire a technical team, including developers and engineers, to bring their digital product ideas to life. Not only are experienced developers often costly to hire, but the process of recruiting, vetting, and onboarding development talent can be both time-consuming and resource-intensive.

In contrast, no-code platforms empower entrepreneurs with the ability to build functional MVPs by simply dragging and dropping forms, design elements, and other pre-built components, all without writing a single line of code. By removing the complexity of traditional software development, no-code tools put product creation within reach for anyone with a vision and an entrepreneurial spirit.

1.1.2 Emphasizing Speed and Flexibility

Startup success often hinges on the ability to iterate rapidly, learn from user feedback, and pivot in response to shifting market conditions. Traditionally, this process could take months, if not years, as teams of developers manually coded each new feature or improvement. However, a no-code MVP allows you to streamline the development process and prioritize speed and flexibility.

By leveraging the power of no-code tools, you can quickly create a working prototype of your digital product, gather user feedback, and make changes or additions accordingly. This approach enables you to remain agile and responsive to changing market conditions or advancements in technology, helping to keep your startup ahead of the curve.

1.1.3 Creating Room for Experimentation

In the world of startups, ideas are like seeds, sometimes growing into successful ventures, sometimes withering away. With the no-code movement, entrepreneurs can be more adventurous in their experimentation, exploring multiple potential MVPs simultaneously or rapidly pivoting their ideas as they gather user feedback and better understand the evolving landscape.

The reduced time and cost associated with developing no-code MVPs means that you can afford to take more risks and potentially uncover a true game-changer that would have remained unexplored in a more traditional development environment.

1.1.4 Democratizing Innovation

The no-code revolution levels the playing field for aspiring entrepreneurs and innovators, offering a more inclusive environment for anyone with a great idea to make their mark. Previously, aspiring entrepreneurs who lacked technical skills faced a significant disadvantage in bringing their digital products to the market. However, with the rise of no-code tools, these individuals can now pursue their dreams without the need for programming expertise.

This democratization of innovation is leading to a more diverse array of digital products that cater to different markets, ultimately benefiting both startup companies and consumers alike.

1.1.5 Learning the Principles of No-Code MVP Development

As you continue on this no-code MVP journey, you'll discover the fundamental principles and strategies for utilizing these powerful tools and platforms to their fullest potential. Using real-world examples and case studies, we will illustrate how no-code tools can be used to build robust MVPs that garner the attention of customers and investors alike. You'll learn how to identify core features, validate user experiences, and optimize your MVP for success.

In the end, the combination of powerful no-code tools and a solid understanding of the MVP development process will provide you with the skills necessary to launch your startup ideas into the digital realm and ultimately change the trajectory of your entrepreneurial journey.

1.1 Embracing the No-Code Movement

In today's fast-paced digital world, entrepreneurs and innovators are constantly on the lookout for ways to quickly build, test, and iterate their ideas. The traditional approach of investing significant time and resources into developing custom software solutions from scratch is not only time-consuming and expensive but also comes with a high risk of failure due to unforeseen challenges and assumptions.

Enter the "No-Code Movement" - a groundbreaking new approach to building and validating Minimum Viable Products (MVPs) quickly, with little to no coding knowledge. This movement is fueled by the rise of powerful no-code platforms and tools that enable non-technical users to create fully-functional web and mobile applications, using visual interfaces and pre-built components.

In this section, we'll explore the key benefits of no-code MVPs and how they empower startups and innovators to bring their ideas to life without the need for extensive technical skills or resources. We'll also touch upon the various no-code tools and platforms available, and provide guidance on how to choose the most suitable option for your specific needs.

1.1.1 Faster Time-to-Market

One of the most compelling reasons for using no-code MVPs is their potential to dramatically reduce the time it takes to bring a product to market. By leveraging pre-built components and visual development environments, you can quickly build and deploy functional applications in a matter of weeks or even days, as opposed to the months or years it would take with custom development.

This faster time-to-market means you can get your ideas out in the hands of users quickly, gather valuable feedback, and iterate rapidly in response to real-world user insights. This agility is essential for startups looking to establish themselves in competitive markets, where every second counts and being the first to market with an innovative solution can make or break your business.

1.1.2 Lower Costs and Resource Requirements

The cost of custom software development can be staggering, especially for startups and small businesses with limited budgets. By eliminating the need to hire expensive developers or invest in specialized technical skill sets, no-code MVPs significantly reduce upfront costs and resource requirements.

No-code platforms offer affordable subscription plans or pay-as-you-go pricing models, making it feasible for businesses of all sizes to access powerful development tools without breaking the bank. Additionally, the reduced coding complexity makes it easier to maintain and update your

MVP, further driving down long-term costs while ensuring your product always stays current.

1.1.3 Democratization of Innovation

One of the most transformative aspects of the no-code movement is the democratization of app development, allowing people from diverse backgrounds and with varying technical expertise to build and launch their own products. By removing the technical barriers to entry, no-code MVPs empower a wider group of innovators to experiment, validate, and iterate on their ideas, creating more possibilities for groundbreaking solutions.

This newfound creative freedom fosters a more inclusive and diverse landscape for innovation, where the best ideas can rise to the top, regardless of the creator's technical prowess. The no-code movement thus holds immense potential for unlocking untapped talent and driving meaningful change across various industries.

1.1.4 Experimentation and Iteration

With the ability to quickly deploy and test no-code MVPs, entrepreneurs can now adopt a lean startup methodology and embrace a culture of experimentation. No-code platforms make it simple to iterate on your MVP in response to user feedback or market changes, promoting a more data-driven and adaptive approach to product development.

This increased flexibility enables startups to refine their core value proposition, optimize user experiences, and ultimately drive product-market fit, all while minimizing the risk and cost traditionally associated with pivoting or making significant product updates.

1.1.5 Choosing the Right No-Code Platform

As the no-code movement gains momentum, the market is becoming crowded with options, making it essential for startups to carefully evaluate and choose the right platform for their needs. Some popular no-code platforms include Bubble, Webflow, Adalo, Appgyver, and Glide, among others.

When comparing platforms, consider factors such as:

- Platform capabilities: Does the platform support the functionality and complexity required for your MVP?
- Integration options: Ensure that the platform can connect with the third-party services and APIs you plan to use.
- Pricing and scalability: Look for affordable pricing plans and the ability to scale your app as your business grows.
- Community and support: Seek platforms with active communities and robust support resources, which can help you troubleshoot issues and learn best practices.

In conclusion, the no-code movement has the potential to profoundly disrupt the way startups and innovators build and validate their ideas. By embracing no-code MVPs, businesses can accelerate time-to-market, reduce costs, democratize innovation, and foster a culture of experimentation and iteration. As you embark on your journey with no-code MVPs, use the insights and guidance provided in this book to make informed decisions and set yourself up for success.

1.1 The Age of No-Code: Embracing a New Way of Building MVPs

When it comes to launching a successful startup, time is of the essence. Dozens of new ideas are birthed every day, and there's always the risk that someone is already working on the same concept. Moreover, investors and customers are always eager to see something tangible they can evaluate, test, and use in order to decide whether the startup is worth their time and resources. This brings us to the MVP, or the Minimum Viable Product.

Traditionally, building an MVP involved hiring developers, writing codes, designing a user interface, and sometimes even more. This not only takes a considerable amount of time but also requires a hefty budget. But what if there's a way to circumvent these time-consuming and costly processes? Enter the world of No-Code MVPs.

No-code tools have become increasingly popular as a faster, more efficient, and less expensive alternative to traditional application development methods. These tools enable founders and even non-technical entrepreneurs to streamline the process of building an MVP, allowing them to validate their ideas and share them with the world as quickly as possible.

1.1.1 No-Code MVP: What Exactly Is It?

In simple terms, a No-Code Minimum Viable Product (MVP) is an early-stage iteration of a product or solution, built using no-code tools and platforms. No-code MVPs enable founders to create applications without writing a single line of code. Instead, these platforms offer drag-and-drop functionality, visual app-building editors, and pre-built templates that help founders build and customize their products in a matter of hours or days.

1.1.2 The Advantages: Why No-Code?

1. **Speed**: No-code tools and platforms deliver an unprecedented level of speed to the MVP development process. Entrepreneurs can validate their ideas and bring them to market in a fraction of the time it would take using traditional development methods.
2. **Reduced Costs**: No-code technology eliminates the need for costly software development and infrastructure, allowing founders to save a significant amount on their budgets. The rise of no-code platforms has made it possible even for bootstrapped startups to build their MVPs without breaking the bank.
3. **Collaboration & Flexibility**: No-code platforms enable a more collaborative and flexible environment, allowing cross-functional teams to work on an MVP in parallel. Product managers, designers, marketers, and developers can iterate together, share feedback, and modify the product as needed.
4. **Empowering Non-Technical Founders**: One of the biggest game-changers of the no-code movement is that it democratizes the opportunity to bring an idea to life. Founders who lack technical skills can now build MVPs for their business without relying on a developer or technical co-founder.
5. **Easy Scaling and Modification**: No-code platforms usually come with built-in integrations that make scaling easier. As your MVP evolves, it's simple to add features, modify existing ones, and integrate additional tools and services, accommodating the ever-changing and growing demands of your startup.

1.1.3 Top No-Code Tools and Platforms You Should Know

There is a myriad of no-code tools and platforms available today, with more coming up all the time. Here's a quick rundown of some popular no-code platforms, which excel in different areas:

1. **Webflow**: Webflow is a powerful platform for designing and launching responsive websites without writing any code. It enables users to craft custom, visually-appealing, and high-quality website designs from scratch.
2. **Bubble**: Bubble is a popular platform for building web applications through a simple drag-and-drop interface. It features a visual editor and a vast library of plugins that can help you create complex and rich web applications without writing any code.
3. **Appgyver**: This platform allows users to create mobile, desktop, and web applications using a responsive visual interface, along with an extensive variety of integrations and functionalities.
4. **Zapier**: Zapier is an automation tool that connects various apps and services without the need for any custom code. It's instrumental in creating automated workflows and triggers between platforms, making it easier to integrate and manage data across multiple applications.
5. **Airtable**: Airtable is a flexible and user-friendly database tool that allows you to create custom databases, manage spreadsheets, and connect with other tools in your stack, all without requiring any coding knowledge.

1.1.4 Ready, Set, Build: How to Create Your First No-Code MVP

Building a No-Code MVP requires a thoughtful process where you map out your idea, break it down into smaller components, and organize these components in a way that best suits your intended user experience. The following steps can guide you through this process:

1. **Define**: Clearly define the problem you're looking to solve and identify your target audience. This will help you ensure your MVP caters to the needs and interests of your potential customers.
2. **Research**: Analyze your competition and evaluate the landscape of your industry, this will provide insights into the must-have features for your MVP and showcase the unique value proposition that will set you apart from existing solutions.
3. **Sketch**: Brainstorm and sketch out the main user flows and wireframes for your MVP. This will help you visualize the user journey, organize your thoughts and ideas, and ensure that you're building a user-centric solution.
4. **Select**: Choose the right no-code tools and platforms that best suit your MVP's requirements. You may need to mix and match different services to cover all your bases effectively.
5. **Build**: Use the selected platforms to create your MVP, taking care to adhere to the features and user flows defined earlier in the process. Test the solution as you go to eliminate any potential issues.
6. **Iterate**: As soon as your MVP is live, gather user feedback, iterate on your solution, and fine-tune your offering based on the insights you gain. The ability to quickly and easily iterate is one of the essential benefits of no-code MVPs.

In conclusion, embracing the power of no-code MVPs can lead to success in the fast-paced world of startups. The time and resources saved, the quick iterations and seamless scalability, and the ability for non-technical founders to bring their ideas to life all point to the future - the age of no-code.

The Power of No-Code MVPs

Why Every Entrepreneur Needs a No-Code MVP

In today's fast-paced, hyper-competitive business landscape, aspiring entrepreneurs often face a dilemma. They have a potentially world-changing idea for a product or service, but lack the necessary resources – particularly time and technical expertise – to bring it to life.

Enter the No-Code Minimum Viable Product (MVP). With the help of no-code platforms, anyone, regardless of their coding abilities, can now build powerful digital solutions tailored to their unique needs, all without touching a single line of code.

In this section, we will explore the fundamental concept of No-Code MVPs and discuss the numerous advantages that make them an indispensable tool for today's entrepreneurs. From speed and flexibility to cost-effectiveness and continuous learning, this new breed of MVPs offers invaluable benefits – especially for startups with limited resources and demanding timelines.

Defining No-Code Minimum Viable Products

Before we delve into the advantages of No-Code MVPs, let's take a quick look at the two key concepts in this equation – MVPs and no-code development.

- **Minimum Viable Product (MVP)**: An MVP is a version of a new product with the minimum features required to capture the core functionalities and value propositions while attracting early adopters. This stripped-down version of the product allows startups to test the waters, gather user feedback, and iterate based on data-driven decisions – all without spending valuable resources on developing a full-featured, polished product. In short, an MVP enables startups to fail fast, learn quickly, and pivot if necessary.

- **No-Code Development**: No-code tools are visual development platforms that allow users to create apps, websites, and digital products without writing any code. Instead, they use drag-and-drop interfaces, pre-built templates, and preconfigured components to build the desired functionalities. No-code platforms democratize the app development process, enabling non-technical users – such as entrepreneurs, business analysts, and designers – to turn their ideas into working prototypes quickly and cost-effectively, all without relying on scarce developer resources or extensive technical expertise.

Now that we have a basic understanding of these two concepts, we can appreciate the true power of No-Code MVPs: a synthesis of the lean and practical approach of MVPs with the agility and accessibility of no-code tools. This powerful combination allows startups to test, validate, and iterate on their ideas swiftly, with minimal risk and investment.

Advantages of No-Code MVPs for Startups

1. **Speed of Execution**: No-code platforms dramatically reduce the time it takes to build a functional MVP. With an intuitive drag-and-drop interface, guided development processes, and pre-built modules, entrepreneurs can quickly bring their ideas to life – sometimes in a matter of hours or days, rather than

weeks or months. This allows founders to focus on validating their hypothesis and iterating to achieve product-market fit at a much faster pace.

2. **Lower Development Costs**: By bypassing the need to hire developers, no-code MVPs significantly cut down on upfront costs – a lifesaver for cash-strapped startups. Besides, no-code platforms often offer a subscription-based pricing model, which allows you to only pay for what you need, and upgrade or downgrade as your requirements change.

3. **Ease of Iteration**: The agile nature of no-code solutions makes it easy to make changes, updates, and refinements to your MVP based on real-time user feedback. This invaluable feature empowers startups to correct course and optimize their product offerings without having to restart from scratch or undertake a costly, time-consuming development cycle.

4. **Flexibility and Customizability**: No-code tools come with a vast array of options, integrations, and extensions, offering startups the flexibility to create the exact solution they need – all without any coding or technical expertise. You can choose from a library of ready-to-use modules, or even build custom components to meet your specific requirements.

5. **Collaboration and Accessibility**: No-code platforms offer a level playing field for startups with diverse, cross-functional teams. They promote collaboration and communication among members by providing a unified, visual platform where everyone can contribute to the development of the product – from ideation to execution.

By harnessing the power of No-Code MVPs, entrepreneurs can quickly and efficiently test their ideas, gather crucial feedback, and pivot their startup in the right direction – all while saving time, money, and resources. In the following chapters, we'll provide you with a step-by-step guide to building your own No-Code MVP and setting your startup on the path to success.

1.1 Embracing the No-Code Movement

Gone are the days when launching a startup required a deep understanding of coding, a dedicated team of developers, or thousands of dollars to outsource your development work. The emergence of the no-code movement has led to a simpler, faster, and more cost-effective way to bring your ideas to life.

No-Code MVPs represent a quickly growing trend in the world of entrepreneurship, enabling founders and startup enthusiasts to bring their business ideas to life with minimal technical knowledge. By leveraging the power of no-code platforms and tools, potential entrepreneurs can now create and iterate their Minimum Viable Product (MVP) in a matter of days or weeks, rather than months or years.

In this section, we'll explore the power of no-code MVPs and why they have become vital to the modern startup ecosystem. You'll discover how these innovative solutions have democratized startup innovation, speeding up the overall process of validating and launching a startup.

1.1.1 The No-Code Ecosystem

The no-code ecosystem is a collection of solutions that enable non-technical users to create, customize, and deploy powerful software applications without writing a single line of code. It consists of a variety of tools, platforms, and services that provide built-in functionalities to develop and customize your applications according to your unique requirements.

Some popular examples include Webflow, Bubble, Zapier, Adalo, Airtable, and many more.

The growing library of no-code tools covers a wide range of categories and functionalities, such as website builders, app builders, data management, automation tools, and even full-fledged development platforms.

The main goal of these no-code solutions is to empower individuals or teams with little to no technical background to create fully functional software applications, essentially lowering the barrier to entry for entrepreneurs who want to validate their startup ideas or innovate quickly.

1.1.2 The Benefits of No-Code MVPs

Nowadays, creating, validating, and iterating on an MVP has become an essential part of startup ideation and growth. The MVP allows entrepreneurs to quickly test and analyze their product or service, enabling them to make necessary adjustments or pivots before investing further time, effort, or resources. No-code MVPs, in particular, offer several advantages:

1. **Speed**: No-code tools are designed to be user-friendly and straightforward, making it possible to build your MVP at an astonishingly rapid pace. You can construct prototypes, carry out tests, and iterate on your ideas within days or weeks, instead of lengthy development cycles.
2. **Flexibility**: With a comprehensive range of no-code tools available, entrepreneurs can mix and match various solutions to create an MVP that's precisely tailored to their unique needs. They can also ease into adapting their product as their startup evolves, without incurring significant delays or costs.

3. **Cost-Effective**: No-code MVPs eliminate the need for hiring developers or outsourcing your product development to external agencies. This means once you learn to navigate the no-code landscape, your costs drastically decrease while still retaining the ability to build and iterate on exceptional products.
4. **Validation**: The ultimate goal of an MVP is to validate your startup idea among potential customers. The faster you can build and iterate on your MVP, the quicker you can get feedback and uncover insights about your target market, helping you steer your startup in the right direction.
5. **Risk Reduction**: Building a no-code MVP minimizes the risks associated with building a full product right from the start. You can test your ideas, garner traction, or discover potential roadblocks without incurring significant financial or time investment.

1.1.3 No-Code Processes and Workflow

Developing a no-code MVP usually follows a well-defined process and workflow structured around a series of steps:

1. **Ideation**: The first step is to define your startup idea, identify your target audience, and the problem you intend to solve. It's essential to clarify who your users will be and how your solution will bring value to their lives.
2. **MVP Planning**: Once you have a solid understanding of your idea, the next step is to determine the essential features, functionalities, and user flows that best represent a minimal viable version of your product. Prioritize these features to build an achievable MVP scope.
3. **Choosing No-Code Tools**: Depending on the nature of your MVP, the features it should have, and your

own preferred workflow, you'll need to choose the right no-code tools that cater to your requirements. This may involve selecting from website builders, app builders, automation tools, or other specialized platforms.

4. **Building the MVP**: With your plan in place, begin constructing your MVP using the chosen no-code tools. Ensure that the essential features and user flow patterns are well-represented and functional.

5. **Testing and Validation**: Once the MVP is built, it's time to gather user feedback, conduct testing, and identify potential gaps or issues that need addressing. Reassess your assumptions and validate whether your solution is on the right track.

6. **Iterating and Improving**: Use the insights gained from testing and validation to make necessary adjustments, enhancements, or pivots to your MVP. This iterative process makes it easier to make timely changes, realigning your startup as needed.

As you can see, no-code MVPs have revolutionized the world of entrepreneurship, streamlining and accelerating the process of building, validating, and iterating on your ideas to maximize your chances of success. By embracing the no-code movement, you can position your startup for rapid growth while maintaining your focus on innovation and value creation.

2. The No-Code Toolkit: Essential Platforms and Tools

2.1 Essential Platforms for Building No-Code MVPs

Building a no-code MVP is an essential step toward validating your startup idea, and having the right tools is of utmost importance to get started on the right foot. In this chapter, we will discuss the essential platforms that can help you build your no-Code MVP with minimum technical knowledge.

2.1.1 Webflow

Webflow is a powerful design and development platform that allows you to create responsive websites without writing a single line of code. It combines an intuitive drag-and-drop interface with a complete set of design tools that can help you build and customize your MVP with ease.

Webflow features:

- Responsive design without complex media queries
- Custom animations and interactions
- A vast library of pre-built components and elements
- Visual CMS to manage your content dynamically
- Hosting optimized for speed and performance
- Collaboration tools to work with team members

2.1.2 Bubble

Bubble is a no-code platform that allows you to build custom web applications from scratch. With Bubble, you can design, develop, and deploy fully functional web apps without any programming knowledge.

Bubble features:

- Drag-and-drop visual builder
- Customizable UI elements (buttons, inputs, etc.)
- Database management system

- Connect to external APIs and services
- Custom logic and workflows
- Integration with popular tools (like Stripe for payments)
- Free hosting with the option to use custom domains

2.1.3 Glide

Glide is a no-code platform that allows you to create mobile applications using Google Sheets as your backend. You can turn any Google Sheet into a beautiful, easy-to-use app and update your app in real-time by editing your Google Sheet.

Glide features:

- Customizable app templates
- Google Sheets powered backend
- Display, filter, and sort data in various layouts
- Custom actions (buttons, forms, etc.) to interact with your data
- Available for both Android and iOS
- No installation required – share via a URL

2.1.4 Adalo

Adalo is another no-code platform that enables you to create custom mobile and web apps. It offers a straightforward, drag-and-drop interface and allows you to build applications with multiple screens, components, and features without any coding knowledge.

Adalo features:

- Drag-and-drop visual editor
- Custom components and UI elements
- Customizable app logic and workflows

- Integration with popular tools (like Stripe for payments)
- Built-in data backend and authentication
- Publish to both Android and iOS app stores
- Personalized branding and custom domain

2.1.5 Zapier

Zapier is a no-code automation platform that connects different web applications and services. It enables you to create automated workflows called "Zaps" by integrating various apps without writing any code.

Zapier features:

- Integration with over 3000 apps and services
- Pre-built Zaps to automate common tasks
- Customizable triggers and actions for your workflows
- Conditional logic to create complex automations
- Scheduled automations to run at predetermined intervals
- Multiple Zaps and Steps to combine different apps and actions

2.2 Essential Tools for No-Code MVPs

In addition to the platforms mentioned above, there are several essential tools that can assist you in various aspects of building your no-code MVP. These tools can save you time, effort, and resources while creating an effective and efficient MVP.

2.2.1 Loom

Loom is a video messaging tool that makes it simple and quick to create and share video messages. It can be instrumental in communicating with your team or including video tutorials and demos with your MVP.

Loom features:

- Instant video recording with a single click
- Screen sharing with voice narration
- Chrome extension for quick access
- Video annotation and drawing tools
- Instant video sharing via a URL
- Integration with popular tools like Slack, Notion, and Trello

2.2.2 Typeform

Typeform is a web-based form and survey builder that enables you to create interactive and engaging forms, quizzes, and surveys for your MVP. It can be used for collecting user feedback, lead generation, registration, and more.

Typeform features:

- Intuitive drag-and-drop form builder
- Customizable question types and form logic
- Embeddable forms and popups for your website
- Custom branding and design
- Integration with popular tools and services
- Analytics and insights for your form data

2.2.3 Canva

Canva is a graphic design platform with an extensive library of templates, images, and design elements for creating professional graphics and visuals for your MVP. It can help you create logos, presentations, social media graphics, and more.

Canva features:

- Easy-to-use drag-and-drop interface
- Templates for various design types
- A massive library of stock images and design elements
- Customizable typography and color palettes
- Collaboration tools for team projects
- Export in multiple file formats

2.2.4 Airtable

Airtable is a powerful spreadsheet-meets-database platform that lets you create custom databases, organize data, and collaborate with your team. It can be used for project management, CRM, content planning, and more.

Airtable features:

- Customizable table templates
- Advanced filtering, sorting, and grouping options
- Different data types and field types
- Real-time collaboration and team permissions
- Integration with popular tools and services
- API for connecting with other platforms

By leveraging these essential platforms and tools, you can quickly and effectively build, test, and validate your startup idea with a no-code MVP. Embrace the power of no-code, and watch your idea grow into a successful venture.

2. The No-Code Toolkit: Essential Platforms and Tools

The no-code movement has spawned a rich ecosystem of platforms and tools that allow anyone with an idea to create and validate startup ideas quickly. With these tools, you no longer need to be a developer or have technical expertise to build a web application, mobile app, or even a full-fledged product.

In this section, we'll explore some of the essential platforms and tools that will equip you with everything you need to create your minimum viable product (MVP) without writing a single line of code. We'll categorize the tools based on their purpose in the no-code development process, from ideation to prototype to launch.

A. Idea Validation and Customer Research

Before starting on the development of your no-code MVP, you need to validate your idea and gather insights about your target customers.

1. **Google Forms** - A free, versatile tool for creating and sharing surveys, quizzes, and forms. Use it to gather customer feedback, conduct market research, or measure user satisfaction.
2. **Typeform** - A powerful survey and form builder that creates engaging, conversational experiences for your audience. Typeform provides templates for various purposes, including customer feedback, product validation, and user research.
3. **SurveyMonkey** - An online survey tool that offers a wealth of features, including pre-built survey

templates, data analysis tools, and integrations with third-party applications.

B. Visual Design and Prototyping

Collaborate with your team to create visuals, wireframes, and interactive prototypes with these design tools:

1. **Figma** - A popular web-based vector design tool that allows you to design, prototype, and collaborate in real-time. It comes with a library of UI elements, making it easy to create and test user interfaces.
2. **Adobe XD** - A powerful design and prototyping tool from Adobe that enables you to design, prototype, and share interactive experiences. It is packed with a rich set of tools, including UI elements, components, and plugins.
3. **Sketch** - A popular design tool for Mac users, known for its simplicity, efficiency, and integrative capabilities. With a massive library of plugins, Sketch enables you to design user interfaces and prototype interactive experiences.

C. Web App and Website Builders

No-code website builders make it easy to create responsive, visually-appealing websites without writing any code.

1. **Webflow** - A web design and hosting platform that allows you to design, build, and launch responsive websites visually. With its built-in CMS, you can create and manage content without writing any code.
2. **Wix** - A drag-and-drop website builder with a wide selection of design templates and 3rd party app integrations. Wix also offers an integrated

eCommerce platform, making it easy to set up an online store.

3. **Squarespace** - A popular platform for creating beautiful websites, portfolio sites, and online stores. Squarespace offers a sleek, modern design aesthetic and a range of powerful tools to customize your site's appearance and functionality.

D. Mobile App Builders

Create native mobile apps for iOS and Android without writing any code using these no-code mobile app builders.

1. **Adalo** - A no-code mobile app builder that allows you to create and launch native mobile apps on iOS and Android. Adalo's visual interface allows you to build apps quickly and intuitively.
2. **Thunkable** - A drag-and-drop app development platform that enables you to build fully-functional native apps for iOS and Android. It offers a wide range of components and an extensive library of pre-built templates for UI and layout design.
3. **OutSystems** - A powerful low-code platform for building enterprise-grade mobile and web applications. Its visual development environment and integration capabilities make it easy to create complex apps with minimal coding.

E. eCommerce Platforms

Launch and manage your online store with these no-code eCommerce platforms.

1. **Shopify** - A leading eCommerce platform that allows you to create, manage, and grow your online store. With a wide range of pre-built templates, plugins, and

third-party integrations, you can create a custom-tailored shopping experience for your customers.

2. **BigCommerce** - An all-in-one eCommerce platform that offers device-agnostic design templates, advanced marketing tools, and support for various payment gateways. It's a scalable solution for businesses of all sizes.
3. **WooCommerce** - A powerful, customizable, and free eCommerce platform that integrates with WordPress. It offers a wide range of plugins and themes, allowing you to create a fully-customized online store.

F. Workflow Automation and Integration

No-code workflow automation tools help you automate tasks and integrate different platforms to create a seamless user experience.

1. **Zapier** - A popular workflow automation tool that connects different applications and services, enabling you to automate tasks without writing any code. It supports thousands of integrations, making it easy to create complex workflows.
2. **Integromat** - A visual workflow automation platform that allows you to connect and automate tasks between different applications. Its drag-and-drop interface makes it easy to create custom integrations and automated workflows.
3. **IFTTT** - A lightweight, user-friendly automation platform that connects and automates tasks between popular applications and services, using "if this, then that" logic.

In conclusion, the no-code landscape offers an abundance of tools for non-technical founders to build and validate their startup ideas swiftly. This is by no means an exhaustive list;

however, this toolkit is an excellent starting point for anyone looking to build an MVP with zero or minimal coding experience. Embrace the power of no-code, and turn your idea into a reality!

A. Overview of the No-Code Toolkit

In this section, we will take a deep dive into the essential platforms and tools that form the backbone of every no-code MVP. These tools have been carefully selected to save you time, effort, and money in the entire process of bringing your startup ideas to life. They cater to a diverse set of requirements, ranging from designing and building your web and mobile applications to automating complex workflows, gathering user feedback, and even managing your customer base without writing a single line of code.

Each platform and tool listed in this toolkit takes care of a specific aspect of building and launching your no-code MVP. By the time you're done with this section, we hope you'll be armed with a comprehensive understanding of which tools to choose based on your product requirements and target audience.

Now, let's take a closer look at these essential platforms and tools in the no-code toolkit:

1. No-Code Development Platforms

These are comprehensive tools that allow you to build, design, and launch your web or mobile application without any coding experience. They often feature a what-you-see-is-what-you-get (WYSIWYG) interface, making it easy for you to visualize and create your ideal product. Some popular no-code development platforms include:

- **Bubble**: A powerful and versatile platform for building web applications. Bubble's key features include an intuitive visual editor, built-in database management, a vast collection of plugins, and direct API integrations.
- **Webflow**: An all-in-one design and development platform that focuses on creating visually stunning and fully responsive websites. Webflow is known for its easy-to-use interface and real-time editing capabilities.
- **Adalo**: A mobile app development platform that helps you design, build, and launch custom native apps for Android and iOS devices. The easy-to-use drag-and-drop interface makes the process of building an app quick and effortless.
- **OutSystems**: A low-code platform that offers an extensive collection of pre-built templates and resources, perfect for creating enterprise-grade mobile and web applications on the fly. OutSystems supports integration with leading database and analytics tools, making it a popular choice among larger organizations.

2. Workflow Automation Tools

Once you've built your MVP, the next step is to automate and streamline business processes without writing any code. Workflow automation tools help you create complex workflows and integrate different no-code tools and platforms seamlessly. Some popular workflow automation tools include:

- **Zapier**: A powerful automation tool that connects and automates over 3,000 applications, featuring an extensive library of pre-built 'Zaps' to help you get started quickly.

- **Integromat**: A versatile automation platform that combines a visual interface with support for API-based integrations. Integromat provides an extensive suite of functions and tools to create complex workflows and processes with ease.
- **n8n.io**: An open-source node-based workflow automation tool that allows you to set up custom integrations and automate tasks across multiple platforms and services.

3. User Data Collection and Feedback

Gathering user feedback is essential when it comes to validating your startup idea and improving your product. Here are some tools to help you collect data and feedback from your users:

- **Google Forms**: A simple yet powerful survey and form builder that comes with the Google suite. It includes various question types, response validation, and automatic collection of data into a Google Sheet.
- **Typeform**: A user-centric form and survey builder with a focus on user experience. Typeform offers engaging, interactive, and easily customizable forms that can be embedded into your website or shared via a unique URL.
- **Hotjar**: A vital tool for understanding user behavior on your website, featuring heatmaps, session recordings, and conversion funnel analysis. Hotjar also allows you to collect user feedback through surveys and polls.

4. Customer Relationship Management (CRM) Tools

Managing your customer base and keeping track of their needs and preferences is essential in the early stages of your startup. CRM tools help you manage, analyze, and improve your customer relationships without any coding skills. Some popular CRM tools include:

- **Airtable**: A versatile no-code platform that combines the power of spreadsheets and databases, allowing you to create everything from project management boards to custom CRM systems.
- **Streak**: A CRM tool built directly into your Gmail account, Streak offers a simple and lightweight solution for managing your customer relationships seamlessly within your existing email inbox.
- **HubSpot CRM**: A comprehensive CRM platform with out-of-the-box marketing, sales, and customer service tools. HubSpot CRM is easy to use and offers a wide range of integrations, making it suitable for startups of all sizes.

With a deep understanding of these essential platforms and tools in your no-code toolkit, you're now ready to start building and validating your startup ideas quickly and efficiently. The power of no-code MVPs is now at your fingertips. Good luck!

2.2 The No-Code Toolkit: Essential Platforms and Tools

In this subsection, we will explore the essential platforms and tools that form the backbone of the no-code movement. These tools and platforms enable budding entrepreneurs, product managers, and visionaries to focus on quickly building and validating their startup ideas, without spending months on development.

2.2.1 Visual Development Platforms

Visual development platforms allow building web and mobile applications using a visual interface, bypassing the need to write code manually. These platforms typically use a drag and drop interface, which allows users to create UIs and develop application logic using pre-built components. Some popular visual development platforms include:

1. **Webflow**: A powerful website and application builder that allows users to create, design, and develop responsive websites visually. Webflow's more advanced features include database integration, user authentication, and the ability to integrate custom code snippets. The platform also seamlessly handles web hosting and optimizes site performance with content delivery networks (CDNs).
2. **Bubble**: A versatile platform for building web applications from scratch or using customizable templates. Bubble enables users to create complex logic and workflows, without writing code. Bubble also provides database management capabilities and supports third-party integrations using APIs.
3. **Wix**: A well-known and intuitive website builder, empowering users to create custom websites through its wide variety of design templates and drag-and-drop editor. Wix offers essential features like e-commerce setup, user authentication, and third-party integrations, catering to various business needs.

2.2.2 Automation Tools

Automation tools are crucial for connecting different platforms, databases, and applications to create a seamless flow of information between various systems. These tools foster efficiency and enable users to create powerful automated workflows, without writing code. Some popular automation tools include:

1. **Zapier**: A platform that connects thousands of apps and services, enabling users to automate data exchange and create multi-step workflows. Zapier offers conditional logic for further flexibility in creating automation workflows, allowing users to reduce manual work and gain efficiency across their applications.
2. **Integromat**: A powerful automation platform that offers similar functionality as Zapier, with the added benefit of a visually intuitive editor. Integromat's unique point lies in its user interface, where users can create automation workflows using a series of interconnected nodes, making it easier to understand the flow of data and actions.
3. **IFTTT**: An easy-to-use automation service that allows users to create simple, yet effective rules referred to as "Applets." IFTTT connects multiple platforms and devices, letting users automate tasks in IoT, smart home devices, and web applications.

2.2.3 Database and Backend Solutions

Creating applications usually requires a robust and secure database to store and manage data. The following database and backend solutions are no-code friendly and offer customizable features to suit diverse project requirements:

1. **Airtable**: A cloud-based database platform merging the functionality of spreadsheets with the power of relational databases, allowing users to create versatile and visually appealing databases. Airtable offers an intuitive interface and features like custom views, forms, and API integration.
2. **Xano**: A flexible backend-as-a-service platform enabling users to build complex, scalable, and secure backend infrastructure without writing code. Xano

provides a straightforward editor and robust API management capabilities, allowing users to connect their applications to various data sources.

3. **Firebase**: A comprehensive backend platform by Google, offering a variety of services such as real-time databases, user authentication, machine learning, and analytics. Firebase's integration with no-code platforms like Bubble and Webflow allows users to build applications with powerful backend capabilities effortlessly.

2.2.4 Design and Prototyping Tools

Design and prototyping tools are indispensable for creating visually appealing UIs and efficiently testing UX flows before application development. Some popular design and prototyping tools are listed below:

1. **Figma**: A cloud-based design tool that allows users to create sleek user interfaces and interactive prototypes effortlessly. Figma offers real-time collaboration, making it perfect for team-based design projects.
2. **Sketch**: A popular design tool mainly for Mac users, which offers similar functionality as Figma. Sketch enables users to create UI designs, vector illustrations, and interactive prototypes with ease.
3. **Adobe XD**: A comprehensive design tool by Adobe that integrates seamlessly with other Adobe products, offering the ability to create rich designs and interactive prototypes for web and mobile applications.

These no-code platforms and tools form the foundation for swiftly bringing startup ideas to life, allowing entrepreneurs to focus on validating their concepts and measuring the success of their product idea. By leveraging these tools, stakeholders can evolve and iterate their products rapidly, drastically reducing the time from ideation to market launch.

2.1 Essential Platforms and Tools Every No-Coder Must Know

Before diving deep into examples of no-code MVPs and experimenting with your startup ideas, it's essential to become familiar with the core platforms and tools available in the no-code ecosystem. Understanding the capabilities and limitations of these platforms will enable you to transition from idea to execution seamlessly while saving time and resources.

There are various no-code platforms and tools out there, each serving a different purpose, such as website builders, databases, e-commerce platforms, workflow automation, visual development tools, and more. In this section, we will outline some of the most popular and effective no-code tools that you need to consider for your no-code MVP journey.

2.1.1 Website Builders

1. **Webflow**: Webflow is a popular no-code web design platform that allows you to create responsive websites and manage content without writing any code. You can style elements visually, add animations, create forms, manage all SEO settings, and fully customize your site. The platform provides powerful CMS capabilities allowing you to integrate with other tools like Zapier, and e-commerce features.
2. **Wix**: Wix is an easy-to-use no-code website builder with a user-friendly interface allowing you to create

full-featured websites with an impressive array of customization options. Wix also provides a library of pre-built templates and applications with many third-party integrations available.

2.1.2 Databases

1. **Airtable**: Airtable is a user-friendly database that looks like a spreadsheet but offers more powerful functionalities such as filtering, sorting, data relationships, and data grouping. You can use Airtable as your database or backend to store and manage your essential data and connect it with other no-code platforms and tools using APIs or Zapier integrations.
2. **Google Sheets**: Google Sheets is a widely used cloud-based spreadsheet similar to Microsoft Excel. However, it offers collaboration, automation, and integration features that make it an excellent solution for lightweight database alternatives when working with no-code platforms.

2.1.3 E-commerce platforms

1. **Shopify**: Shopify is a no-code e-commerce platform allowing entrepreneurs to create and customize online stores without any coding. It offers a wide range of features, such as order management, analytics, and marketing tools, along with hundreds of apps and third-party integrations.
2. **Gumroad**: Gumroad is a no-code e-commerce platform specifically designed for creators to sell digital products, memberships, and subscriptions. It allows you to create product landing pages and

manage sales easily, making it a great option for startups focusing on digital products.

2.1.4 Workflow Automation & APIs

1. **Zapier**: Zapier is a powerful no-code tool that allows you to automate and connect different applications without writing any code. With an extensive library of apps, you can create custom workflows that automate repetitive tasks, such as sending emails, managing social media posts, and handling customer data.
2. **Integromat**: Integromat is an alternative to Zapier that provides more advanced features, such as error handling and conditional routing. This no-code platform enables you to visually design and automate processes between different applications without coding.

2.1.5 Visual Development Tools & App Builders

1. **Bubble**: Bubble is a no-code visual development platform that allows you to build web and mobile applications without writing any code. You can design your app's interface using a drag-and-drop editor, create custom data structures, and define workflow automations through a visual programming interface.
2. **Adalo**: Adalo is a no-code app development platform that makes building mobile applications as easy as designing a website. With a straightforward drag-and-drop interface, you can create native mobile applications for iOS and Android without any coding, manage data, and integrate with various API services.

2.1.6 Chatbots & Messaging

1. **Landbot**: Landbot enables you to create chatbots without writing any code. Using a drag-and-drop interface, you can visually design your chatbot's conversation flow, collect user data, and integrate with other applications like CRM or email platforms.
2. **ManyChat**: ManyChat provides a no-code platform for creating Facebook Messenger chatbots with a visual flow builder. You can set up automated messaging sequences, segment your audience, and even create simple bots for your e-commerce store using templates.

These platforms and tools should serve as a starting point for exploring the no-code landscape. Keep in mind that the no-code ecosystem is continuously evolving, and new tools emerge regularly. When selecting a platform or tool, ensure that it meets your business requirements, cost constraints, and scalability needs. Experiment with these tools, familiarize yourself with their capabilities, and let them power your no-code MVP journey.

3. Defining Your Startup Idea: The Problem, Solution, and Target Audience

3.1. Identifying the Core Problem

One of the critical steps in building a successful startup is identifying the core problem you aim to solve. In this sub-section, we'll walk you through the process of determining the problem your startup will tackle, how to craft a unique solution, and the target audience you'll be serving.

Why Problem Identification Matters

In the world of startups, every successful product or service is rooted in addressing a specific problem. Start from solving a problem, and the chances of your startup succeeding will significantly increase. On the other hand, if you build a product without addressing a clear problem, you'll find it much harder to attract users or customers.

Steps to Identify the Core Problem

To define the core problem, consider the following steps:

1. **Identify pain points**: Start by thinking about the challenges or frustrations that you, your friends, or your family face regularly. Keep an open mind and be observant about the issues people around you are dealing with in various aspects of life, from work and relationships to health and finances.
2. **Validate the problem**: Once you've identified a pain point, dig deeper to understand the root cause of the problem. Speak with people who experienced the issue, look up online discussions on the topic, and seek expert advice to gain insight into the problem's size and scope. Ensure that the problem is significant enough to warrant a solution.
3. **Assess existing solutions**: Investigate existing solutions to the problem. Examine their strengths, weaknesses, and gaps. Identify areas where you can innovate and offer value that differentiates your solution from what's currently available.
4. **Refine your problem statement**: Use your insights to craft a clear and concise problem statement. This should be a brief description that articulates the essence of the problem and how it impacts the users experiencing it.

3.2. Crafting a Unique Solution

After defining the core problem, the next step is to devise a unique solution that delivers significant value to the user. Your product or service should address the problem directly and effectively in a way that differentiates it from other available solutions.

Turning Problem Insights into Solutions

Here are some best practices for crafting a unique solution:

1. **Leverage your skills and expertise**: Consider your own skills and knowledge. Drawing from your unique experience can give you an edge in the market.
2. **Innovate**: Don't be afraid to think outside the box. Experiment with new technologies, processes, or business models to create a differentiated solution catered to your target audience.
3. **Simplify**: Focus on simplifying the user experience. Break down the problem into smaller pieces and address them with targeted, easy-to-understand solutions.
4. **Iterate**: Continuously refine and improve your solution. Feedback from early adopters is essential in making the iteration process seamless and effective.

3.3. Defining Your Target Audience

A well-defined target audience is crucial for your startup's success. With a specific audience in mind, you can tailor your product's features and communication strategy accordingly, optimizing your marketing efforts and maximizing your startup's growth potential.

Narrowing Down Your Potential Customers

To define your target audience, follow these steps:

1. **Segment the market**: Start by segmenting the market based on demographics, psychographics, behaviors, or needs. Try to identify patterns or trends that connect the users most affected by the problem.
2. **Conduct user research**: Conduct interviews, surveys, or focus groups with potential customers to gain a deeper understanding of their needs, motivations, and preferences related to the problem.
3. **Develop personas**: Once you've gathered insights about your potential customers, create user personas—fictional characters that represent them. Include details like age, occupation, goals, pain points, and preferences to paint a clear picture of their needs and expectations.
4. **Validate the audience**: Before finalizing your target audience, ensure that it's large enough to sustain your startup's growth. Research market size, industry trends, and growth potential to make an informed decision.

By thoroughly defining your startup idea, the problem it solves, and the solution it offers, you set the stage for a lean and impactful no-code MVP. A well-defined target audience ensures your product resonates with potential customers and increases the likelihood of your startup's success.

In the next chapter, we'll explore how to build a no-code MVP and test it with real users to validate your startup idea quickly and efficiently.

3. Defining Your Startup Idea: The Problem, Solution, and Target Audience

3.1. Identifying the Problem

Before you even begin to think about building a No-Code MVP, it is crucial to clearly identify the problem you're aiming to solve. This is the foundation of your startup and it will guide all the decisions you make moving forward. Start by asking yourself the following questions:

- What is the main problem my startup is trying to solve?
- Is this problem shared by a large enough group of people?
- Are there existing solutions to this problem? If yes, how can I differentiate or improve upon them?

To increase your chances of success, your problem should be one that is not only common, but also urgent or severe. Start by researching the market and talking to potential customers to identify pain points and validate that the problem is worth addressing.

3.2. Crafting a Solid Solution

Once you're confident that you have a clear understanding of the problem, the next step is to design an innovative solution. Be careful not to jump into building features; instead, focus on solving the core problem in a way that is simple and effective for your target audience. This will be the value proposition for your startup.

To develop your solution, consider the following:

- What is the most straightforward way to address the problem?
- How can I make the solution scalable and cost-effective?
- What technology or No-Code tools can I leverage to streamline the process?

Keep in mind that your initial solution will likely evolve as you validate your business idea and gather feedback from your users. The key is to stay lean and agile, focusing on the features and functionality that provide the most value to your users.

3.3. Defining Your Target Audience

Every successful product or service has a well-defined target audience – a specific group of people for whom the solution was designed. The more precisely you can define your target audience, the better you'll be able to tailor your offering and marketing messages to reach the right people.

When defining your target audience, consider:

- Demographics (age, gender, income, education, occupation)
- Geography (country, region, city)
- Psychographics (interests, values, attitudes)
- Behavioral patterns (purchase behavior, online activity, product usage)

To get a deeper understanding of your target audience, you can create user personas – fictional, but detailed characters that represent your ideal customers. Building user personas can help you uncover insights about your audience's needs, preferences, and pain points, allowing you to make better decisions about your No-Code MVP development.

3.4. Putting It All Together: The Value Proposition

With a clear understanding of the problem, solution, and target audience, it's time to formulate your value proposition. This is a concise statement that concisely and convincingly explains why your startup is unique and how it adds value for your customers.

Your value proposition should answer the following questions:

- What is the main benefit of my product or service?
- Who are my target customers, and what are their needs?
- How does my solution differ from existing offerings in the market?
- Why should my target audience choose my solution over alternatives?

Crafting a powerful value proposition is not an easy task, but it's essential to give your startup direction and focus. A strong value proposition will set you apart from competitors, attract customers, and ultimately pave the way for your No-Code MVP success.

3.1 The Problem: Identifying Real Issues

3.1.1 Recognizing a Genuine Need

One of the most critical aspects of defining your startup idea is identifying a real problem that potential customers are experiencing. Remember, people are not necessarily looking for new products or services; they often desire solutions to their issues. As a startup founder, your primary goal is to discover and understand the market's pains and find innovative ways to alleviate them. Here are some useful techniques you can use to recognize a genuine need:

- Research: Delve into industry reports, read academic papers, or join forums related to your sector to gain insights into prevailing issues faced by the target audience.
- Talk to your target audience: Interview actual individuals experiencing the problem. Empathize with the challenges they face, and strive to understand the level of impact on their daily lives.
- Observe user behavior: Analyze and interpret how people are currently responding to the problem. This study will help you comprehend the strategies they use vis-à-vis the tools they lack.

3.1.2 Quantifying the Problem

After identifying and understanding the problem, it is crucial to assess its significance. Accurately quantifying the issue will help you gauge the potential market size of your solution and estimate the future value of your startup.

- Impact: Measure the extent of the problem's reach, whether it affects a person's every day life, an organization's efficiency, or a broader industry.
- Frequency: Determine how often the issue presents itself to better comprehend the urgency and importance of the solution.

- Cost: Estimate the monetary value of the problem in terms of losses incurred or benefits missed, providing a tangible indicator of demand for the solution.

3.2 The Solution: Crafting a Compelling Offer

3.2.1 Generating Ideas

Once you have identified and quantified the problem, it's time to brainstorm innovative solutions. Here are some prompts to help kickstart your creativity:

- Can existing products or services be improved to solve the problem more efficiently?
- Are there any adjacent markets where solutions might be adapted to address the issue?
- Can you integrate cutting-edge technologies to generate a unique solution?

When brainstorming, try to think beyond conventional approaches and foster an environment of idea-generation without judgment, embracing all possible ideas before narrowing them down.

3.2.2 Validating Ideas

Generating multiple solution ideas is excellent, but it's crucial to ensure these ideas are feasible before moving forward. Validate your concepts by considering:

- Uniqueness: Analyze the competition and assess how your idea differentiates from existing solutions.

- Execution: Evaluate the technical and operational feasibility of implementing the idea.
- Market appeal: Verify whether your target audience finds the idea appealing and are willing to pay for it.

3.3 The Target Audience: Defining Your Ideal Customer

3.3.1 Segmentation

Identifying and understanding your target audience enables you to tailor your solution directly to their needs and preferences. Segment the market along various dimensions, such as demographics, psychographics, and behavioral patterns. Here are some key factors to consider:

- Age
- Gender
- Industry
- Job role
- Geographical location
- Income
- Interests and hobbies
- Pain points and needs

3.3.2 Creating Customer Personas

Customer personas are semi-fictional representations of your ideal clients, synthesized from your market research and data. Designing detailed personas can help you:

- Create empathy between the startup team and potential customers.

- Tailor the messaging and branding of your product effectively.
- Test and validate specific features and functionalities based on persona preferences.

When creating customer personas, ensure they are representative of your target audience and consider multiple scenarios for a more comprehensive understanding of the end-users.

3.3.3 Prioritizing Personas

As your startup evolves, catering to every persona is difficult, especially when resources and time are limited. Hence, it is important to prioritize the most valuable and reachable personas. Assess each persona's potential impact on your business, taking into account factors such as:

- Size of the market segment
- Accessibility in terms of marketing and distribution channels
- The willingness and ability to purchase your solution

By focusing on the most crucial customer personas, you can effectively allocate resources and efforts while building a product-market fit.

In conclusion, defining your startup idea comprises a thorough understanding of the problem, crafting a compelling solution, and identifying your ideal customer. By following these crucial steps, you'll be well on your way to building a scalable, successful No-Code MVP that delivers real value to your target audience.

3.1 Identifying the Problem: The Core of Your Startup Idea

Every successful startup is built around solving a problem or addressing a need. Whether you are creating a product or offering a service, it all starts with understanding the problem before diving into the potential solution. As the foundation of your startup, the problem should not only be clear and concise but also must be relevant and important to your target audience.

Why is identifying the problem important?

Defining the problem is crucial because it will lay the groundwork for the rest of your no-code MVP process. It provides a razor-sharp focus on what you are trying to achieve and helps you come up with innovative solutions. It also plays a vital role in defining your target audience and communicating the unique value proposition of your startup.

3.1.1 Understanding the problem

To begin understanding the problem, start by asking yourself these questions:

1. **What is the problem you are trying to solve?** Clearly state the issue that you have identified and provide context on why it is significant.
2. **Who is currently facing this problem?** Identify the people or organizations that are struggling with the issue you want to address.
3. **How are people currently trying to solve this problem?** Analyze existing solutions in the market

and identify the inefficiencies and limitations they have.

You can either write out the answers or create a mind map to visually explore and conceptualize the problem. In any case, make sure to revisit and refine your understanding of the problem throughout the no-code MVP development process.

3.1.2 Validate the problem

Once you have a clear grasp of the problem, it's important to validate it to ensure it's worth investing your time and resources into building a solution. Validating the problem means confirming that the problem indeed exists and affects a substantial audience who's willing to pay for a solution.

To validate the problem, consider the following approaches:

1. **Conduct market research:** Perform extensive research to gather industry data, trends, and reviews from your target audience, competitors, and industry experts.
2. **Talk to potential customers:** Interview your target audience to gain insights into their pain points, needs, and preferences related to the problem.
3. **Test existing solutions:** Use existing products or services that attempt to address the problem to see if they are effective, and where they fall short.
4. **Run surveys and questionnaires:** Collect feedback from potential users on their experiences with the problem and what they expect from an ideal solution.

Validate the problem by collecting concrete evidence that demonstrates its impact and importance to your target audience.

3.2 Crafting the Solution: Your Unique Value Proposition

Now that you have defined and validated the problem, it's time to craft your solution. This is where you'll need to think about what unique value proposition your startup offers to your target audience. In other words, how is your product or service better or different from existing solutions?

3.2.1 Articulating the solution

To clearly and concisely define your solution, answer the following questions:

1. **What is your product or service?** Describe your solution in simple and clear terms.
2. **How does your solution address the problem?** Explain how your product or service helps to solve the problem and relieve pain points.
3. **What makes your solution unique?** Identify the unique attributes, features, or benefits that differentiate your solution from existing options in the market.

Be specific in outlining the key aspects of your solution, as this will help you communicate it with clarity during the further stages of MVP development and marketing.

3.2.2 Refining the solution

Sometimes, your initial solution may not be perfect or even feasible. Therefore, it's essential to refine your solution based on the feedback you receive from your target audience and other stakeholders. Consider running another round of interviews, surveys or even building a basic prototype to gather feedback that will help you improve your solution.

3.3 Identifying Your Target Audience: Who Will Benefit From Your Solution?

A crucial aspect of defining your startup idea is identifying the target audience — the group of people or organizations who will derive the most value from your solution. Your target audience is the group you should focus your marketing and product development efforts on.

3.3.1 Segmenting the audience

When identifying your target audience, it's essential to be as specific as possible by focusing on particular demographics, industries, or other defining characteristics. Consider segmenting your target audience into more granular groups based on:

1. **Demographics:** Age, gender, education level, marital status, etc.
2. **Geographic location:** Country, region, city, or climate.
3. **Psychographics:** Personality traits, values, hobbies, and lifestyle preferences.
4. **Behavioral characteristics:** Spending habits, brand loyalty, product usage patterns, etc.

By segmenting your audience, you'll be better positioned to develop a more effective no-code MVP, tailor your marketing strategies, and communicate the unique value of your solution to a receptive market.

3.3.2 Validating your target audience

Similar to validating the problem, it's essential to validate that the target audience you've identified is actively looking for a solution and is willing to pay for it. Validate your target audience by applying the same methods used for problem validation, such as conducting interviews, running surveys, and studying the competition.

In conclusion, defining your startup idea requires a deep focus on understanding the problem, crafting an innovative solution, and identifying your target audience. As you progress through the no-code MVP development process, be prepared to iterate and refine your startup idea based on feedback and new insights. Remember that startups are dynamic, and constantly adapting to new information is critical for success.

3.1 The Problem: Identifying the Need

One of the most critical aspects of starting any successful business is identifying a problem that needs solving. A problem represents a gap between the current state and a desired state, and your startup idea is your approach to filling that gap with an innovative solution.

To define the problem you are aiming to solve, you can start with the following questions:

- *What pain point or issue are we trying to resolve?* Be specific and concise, as this will help you solidify the problem and make it more relatable.
- *Whose problem is it?* Precisely identifying your target audience will help you understand the scope of the issue and the potential demand for your product or solution.

- *How is the problem currently being addressed?*
  Research the existing landscape to identify
  competitors, complementary offerings, or even
  potential partners.
- *What are the limitations of the existing solutions?*
  These might be cost, efficiency, scalability, or even
  inconvenience. Identifying the shortcomings of current
  solutions will help you understand what customers
  might be looking for in a better alternative.

Remember that not all problems are created equal – some
issues may be experienced daily by a majority of people,
while others may only impact a niche group. Your job is to
determine whether the problem you have identified is
significant enough that people would pay for your proposed
solution.

3.2 The Solution: Proposing Your Innovative Approach

Once you've defined the problem, you can start refining your
startup idea by crafting a unique, viable, and attractive
solution. This involves thinking of creative ways to address
the problem that are superior to existing alternatives. To
strengthen your proposed solution, consider the following
factors:

- *What is your value proposition?* Your value
  proposition is a clear statement of the benefits your
  product or service offers, and it should be the main
  reason prospective customers would choose your
  solution over a competitor's.
- *How is your solution unique or different from existing
  alternatives?* Think about the features and elements

of your product or service that set it apart from other offerings.

- *Are there any barriers to entry for competitors?* Identify any potential competitive advantages you have that would make it difficult for others to replicate your idea.

It's important to remember that your solution doesn't have to be perfect to begin validating your startup idea – the validation process will naturally help you refine and optimize your offering. Start with a minimum viable product (MVP) – the most basic version of your product – and use feedback to iterate and improve as you move forward.

3.3 The Target Audience: Understanding Your Customers

Understanding your target audience is crucial for many reasons, from effectively marketing your product to iterating on and refining your offering based on customer feedback. To identify who exactly you'll be serving, consider the characteristics of those who face the problem you're trying to solve.

Start by answering these questions:

- *Who is most affected by the problem?* This could be a specific demographic, industry, or geographical area.
- *What other attributes do your potential customers share?* This might include their habits, preferences, or values, and will help you better understand their needs and desires.
- *What motivates your target audience?* In other words, what's most important to them when it comes to the problem you're trying to solve?

- *Where can you find your target audience?* Knowing where your target market spends their time – online or offline – will be invaluable when it comes to reaching them with your marketing efforts.

Once you have a clear understanding of your target audience, you can begin to create personas – fictional characters that embody the traits and characteristics of your ideal users. Use these personas as a helpful reference during product development and marketing to ensure your messages resonate with your customers and your solution meets their needs.

In summary, successfully defining your startup idea involves clarifying the problem you're solving, proposing a unique and innovative solution, and identifying your target audience. With these elements in place, you'll have a strong foundation to begin validating your idea and iterating on your MVP to achieve success.

4. Designing a Compelling User Experience: Prototyping and Product Design

###Wireframes and Mockups: Visualizing Your Product

Before diving into no-code tools to start building your prototype, it's crucial to spend time thinking about what your product will look like, feel like, and how your users will interact with it. For that, you need to start with **wireframes and mockups**. These simple, often black-and-white sketches or diagrams will save you countless hours in development as they provide a visual representation of your app or product.

Wireframes

The primary purpose of creating wireframes is to lay out the overall structure and components of your app or product. They are like the "blueprints" for your future prototype. Wireframes offer several benefits:

- They help you visualize in advance what components you'll need for each part of your app or website.
- Since they're not focused on aesthetics, wireframes allow you to concentrate on functionality and interactivity.
- Wireframes are quick to create and easy to update, meaning you can iterate on your design fast and receive feedback as needed.

There are many tools available to create wireframes—both free and paid. Some popular options include Sketch, Figma, Balsamiq Mockups, and Adobe XD. Regardless of which tool you use, remember that the purpose of a wireframe is to lay out the basic elements of your app, not to design the entire thing.

Mockups

While wireframes define the structure and components, mockups add a layer of visuals to these structures. Mockups are more detailed than wireframes and represent the look and feel of your product or app—including colors, typography, icons, and imagery. They're useful for:

- Providing a more realistic representation of your app, making it easier to communicate and share with others

- Helping you identify any inconsistencies in your design and discover potential issues before actual development begins
- Clarifying any assumptions you made about your app's user interface or overall design

Like with wireframes, there are numerous tools available for creating mockups. Some of the popular choices are Sketch, Figma, Adobe XD, and InVision. When creating your mockups, keep in mind that they're meant to give a clear picture of how the final product will look, so take the time to consider each visual aspect carefully.

Creating a User Flow

Once you have created wireframes and mockups, the next step is to map out the user flow: literally, the steps users will take to navigate through your app or product. The main goal of designing user flows is to ensure that your product offers a smooth experience from start to finish.

To create a user flow, follow these steps:

1. **Define the objectives:** Write down the primary goals or tasks users are expected to perform with your app, such as signing up, purchasing a product, or finding information.
2. **List the steps:** For each objective, write down the detailed steps users need to take to accomplish their goals.
3. **Create a flowchart:** Visually represent the user journey by creating a simple flowchart that links each step in the overall process. Use arrows and decision points to indicate connections or branching paths.
4. **Identify potential problems:** Review your flowchart and identify any possible roadblocks, confusing

moments, or unnecessary steps. Look for opportunities to simplify the user experience or make it more intuitive.

Once you have your user flow completed, it's time to connect your wireframes and mockups to create a more complete understanding of your product's design. This interlinked group of documents can be referred to as your product's **UI/UX kit**.

Bringing Your Design to Life: Building an Interactive Prototype

Now that you have a clear understanding of the core components and user experience of your app or product, it's time to make it interactive. An interactive prototype is a vital step in the process of building and validating your startup idea since it allows you to discover and test how your app will function and how users will interact with it. With a functional prototype, you can gather feedback and make necessary changes before committing resources to full development.

When building an interactive prototype, the no-code approach comes in handy. There are numerous no-code tools available to help you quickly build functional prototypes that can be tested on various devices. Some popular no-code prototyping tools include InVision, Framer, Webflow, and Bubble. Each has its attributes and limitations, so make sure you choose the one that best fits your needs.

As you build your prototype using your chosen no-code tool, use your wireframes and UI/UX kit to guide you in adding components and designing the layout, making sure to keep usability and user experience at the forefront of your mind.

Once your prototype is complete, it's time to test it with real users. Share the link to your prototype with a diverse group of individuals and encourage them to explore, interact, and discover any potential issues or areas for improvement. Ideally, you should test your prototype with users who fit within your target audience to get the most accurate and relevant feedback.

Validate and Iterate: Testing Your Prototype and Gathering Feedback

With your prototype in the hands of your testers, your main priority should be gathering and evaluating feedback. Testers may identify hidden problems, suggest improvements, or reveal features essential to their user experience. This feedback will ultimately guide you in refining and iterating on your product design.

When collecting feedback, keep these tips in mind:

- Provide a clear method for users to share their thoughts, such as a feedback form, email address, or chat function.
- Encourage honest feedback, seeking both positive and negative input.
- Avoid leading questions that may skew the results or influence tester opinions.
- Take notes, record observations, and compile your findings for later analysis.

After gathering feedback from your testers, identify the most common or pressing issues, prioritize and categorize them, and start iterating on your design to address these concerns. This process may involve updating wireframes, redesigning mockups, and altering user flows—all the while, keeping the focus on creating a seamless, intuitive user experience that addresses the real pain points, desires, and expectations of your target audience.

Remember, building and validating a startup idea is an ongoing process of learning, iteration, and improvement. To succeed, you must constantly evolve your app or product based on user feedback and changing market conditions. By leveraging the power of no-code tools and techniques, you can swiftly adapt and enhance your prototype, ensuring that you're always on the right path to achieving product-market fit.

4.1 Prototyping and Product Design: Key Steps for Creating a No-Code MVP with Exceptional UX

When building a No-Code MVP (Minimum Viable Product), you're not just trying to create something functional – your aim is to develop an offering so irresistible that users are excited to try it, love using it, and can't wait to tell their friends about it. To achieve this, you must design a product with an exceptional user experience (UX). The following steps will guide you through the process of creating a no-code MVP that delivers just that.

4.1.1 Understand Your Users

Before you even begin designing your MVP, you need to know who you're designing for. Understanding your target audience, their behaviors, preferences, and pain points will enable you to design an offering that truly resonates with them. Start with the following techniques:

- **Personas:** Create fictional characters that represent your ideal users – who they are, what they do, what they care about, and what their goals are.
- **Empathy maps:** Use these to capture users' thoughts, emotions, and experiences, helping you empathize with their needs.
- **User Journey Mapping:** Identify the different stages your users go through when interacting with your product, and the emotions and actions they take during each phase.

4.1.2 Define the Problem

Your MVP should solve a specific problem or meet a clear need for your target audience. To define this:

- Identify the biggest pain points or unmet needs within your user personas' lives.
- Conduct user research, interviews or surveys to validate the problem and to better understand users' perspectives.
- Clearly articulate the problem you're aiming to solve, and build consensus within your team.

4.1.3 Conceptualize Your Solution

Now that you understand your users and their challenges, you can start brainstorming potential solutions. Consider the following:

- Sketch or write down possible features and user flows that address the problem.
- Validate your solution with real users – conduct interviews, analyzing their reactions to determine whether your solution genuinely meets their needs.

- Refine and iterate your solution based on feedback, ensuring it truly addresses users' pain points.

4.1.4 Create Wireframes

Before building your MVP, visualize the final product by creating wireframes. These simple, sketch-like representations display the layout and key features of your app or website.

- Use a no-code wireframing tool to create wireframes for every step of your user flow.
- Ensure your wireframes are focused on user needs and clearly showcase your solution.
- Validate your wireframes with users, incorporating their feedback to improve UX.

4.1.5 Prototype & Test

With wireframes in hand, it's time to convert them into a clickable prototype – a realistic representation of your final product. While full-fledged no-code tools can be used here, consider using a specialized prototyping tool to streamline the process.

- Use a no-code prototyping tool to turn your wireframes into a fully interactive prototype.
- Refine your prototype based on user tests and feedback.
- Iterate on your design, testing and refining until you have a product that users love.

4.1.6 Choose the Right No-Code Tools

There are various no-code tools available for building MVPs, and choosing the right ones is crucial for creating a seamless UX. Consider the following factors when selecting tools:

- Tool capabilities and limitations - ensure chosen tools can handle required features and integrations.
- Cost-effectiveness, scalability, and potential future iterations.
- Community support and online resources for troubleshooting and learning.

4.1.7 Build Your MVP

With a rigorously tested prototype and the right no-code tools, you're ready to build your MVP.

- Use the chosen no-code tools to implement product features, design elements, and user flows.
- Continuously test and iterate during the development process.
- Prepare your MVP for launch (submitting to app stores, deploying your website, etc.).

4.1.8 Gather Feedback & Iterate

Your work doesn't end with the MVP launch. You must continue to gather user feedback, analyze data, and improve your offering.

- Capture user feedback through surveys, interviews, analytics, usability tests, etc.
- Identify areas of improvement or new features that will enhance UX.

- Use the insights gained to update and optimize your MVP, iterating until you've achieved product-market fit.

By following these steps, you'll transform an idea into a compelling no-code MVP that delivers an outstanding user experience, delighting users while bringing your startup idea to life.

4.1. Prototyping and Product Design: A Deep Dive

The design process is an integral part of developing any product, tangible or digital. It's the phase where the concepts and ideas in your head start coming to reality, allowing you to refine and validate the user experience before you invest time and resources building the product. In the "No-Code MVP" approach, prototyping and product design are especially useful to create representational prototypes, that will allow you to iterate and pivot more easily if necessary. In this subsection, we'll dive deeper into the world of prototyping and product design and how they apply to creating compelling user experiences.

4.1.1. Understanding the Goals of Prototyping

The primary goal of prototyping is to create a visual representation of your proposed solution to a specific problem. This early and abstract version of your product encompasses the core features and functions it should ideally provide to users. The prototyping process enables you to quickly generate and test different ideas, and draw insight from it to improve the design. Here are a few specific goals that prototyping can help you achieve:

1. **Visualize your concept**: Developing a prototype offers an opportunity to transform abstract ideas into a visible and tangible form that can be easily understood by others.
2. **Identify flaws and limitations**: Prototyping allows you to discover and fix any shortcomings, including usability issues, before you invest in the actual development process.
3. **Collect feedback**: You can gather feedback from users or stakeholders with your prototype, which can help you further refine your product based on their needs and expectations.
4. **Test different solutions**: With a quick and iterative approach, prototyping enables you to test different solutions or features and evaluate what works best within your product.

4.1.2. Types of Prototypes

Prototypes can be sorted into different categories depending on the level of fidelity, which refers to how detailed and polished the prototype is. Generally, prototypes can be classified into the following types:

1. **Low-Fidelity Prototypes**: These types of prototypes are often simple and rough, ranging from paper sketches to basic wireframes. They're quick and cost-effective to produce, allowing you to explore and iterate ideas rapidly. They're particularly useful in the early stages of design, when you're still identifying and validating core features.
2. **Mid-Fidelity Prototypes**: As the name implies, mid-fidelity prototypes fall between low and high-fidelity ones in terms of detail and polish. They often resemble the final layout or look of the product more closely but may still lack interactivity and branding.

These prototypes can be helpful when you need to present more detailed visuals for stakeholder buy-in or user testing.

3. **High-Fidelity Prototypes**: This type of prototype closely resembles the final product, including the aspects of visual design, interactivity, and responsiveness, allowing for more effective user testing. However, high-fidelity prototypes can be time-consuming and expensive to create, which is why they're typically reserved for the latter stages of the design process when the concept is more refined and clear.

4.1.3. No-Code Prototyping Tools

There are various no-code tools available today that can help you design prototypes without the need for programming knowledge. Here are some popular no-code prototyping tools you can consider:

1. **Figma**: Figma is a web-based collaborative design tool that enables you to create, prototype, and gather feedback in one place. It offers a wide range of features, such as auto-layout, components, and prototyping tools that can help streamline your design process.
2. **Adobe XD**: Adobe XD is a vector-based design tool that provides powerful prototyping features, allowing you to create interactive wireframes and high-fidelity prototypes effortlessly.
3. **Sketch**: Sketch is another popular vector-based design tool used primarily for creating user interfaces. Although it's not a web-based tool like Figma, Sketch offers various plugins and integrations that can help enhance productivity and collaboration.

4. **InVision**: InVision provides a suite of design and prototyping tools that allow you to create and test functional prototypes on various devices. Integrations with tools like Sketch and Photoshop make it even more versatile and powerful.

4.1.4. Steps to Create an Effective Prototype

1. **Define the problem and solution**: Before you jump into design, it's crucial to clearly outline the problem you're addressing and the proposed solution. Create a list of core features that your prototype should encompass to solve the problem effectively.
2. **Choose the right fidelity**: Select the appropriate level of fidelity for your prototype depending on the stage of your design process and the goals you want to achieve. Start with low-fidelity prototypes to explore and refine ideas before moving on to higher fidelity ones.
3. **Sketch out the user flow**: Map the user journey and key touchpoints across different screens, detailing the actions and interactions your users will perform. This will serve as a blueprint for your prototype.
4. **Design the layout and interactions**: Using your chosen no-code prototyping tool, create the layout, visuals, and interactions that define your prototype. Aim for readability, usability, and consistency throughout your design.
5. **Test and iterate**: Once you have a working prototype, conduct user tests to gather feedback and identify any usability issues or flaws. Iterate on the design based on the insights you've gathered from testing to improve the user experience.

In conclusion, prototyping and product design are vital aspects of designing a compelling user experience. By understanding the goals of prototyping, knowing when to use different types of prototypes, and utilizing no-code prototyping tools, you'll be well-equipped to create functional and visually appealing prototypes that can streamline your design process and improve your chances of achieving success with your startup idea.

4.1 Prototyping and Product Design Foundations

Before diving into the prototyping phase, we must understand the fundamentals of designing a compelling user experience. The outcome of this process is an interactive prototype that serves as a visual representation of your idea. But why is this important? A well-designed prototype:

1. Helps you communicate your ideas better
2. Facilitates collaboration with team members and other stakeholders
3. Allows for user testing and validation before investing significant time and resources into development

Great design not only meets user expectations but also goes beyond, delivering experiences that users will love. To achieve this, you need to follow some essential principles of product design and user experience.

4.1.1 Empathy and User-Centered Design

An excellent user experience starts by understanding your target audience – their needs, motivations, and pain points. This approach leads you to design solutions that resonate with your users and solve their problems effectively.

- **Personas**: Create fictional user profiles that represent real-world people who will ultimately use your product. Personas help you understand demographics, behavior patterns, motivations, and goals.
- **User Stories**: Write user stories to describe how users will interact with your product, focusing on the value they will receive from it. This exercise helps you design the essential features that address their problems.
- **User Flows**: Design users' journeys from start to finish, mapping out the possible paths they may take while using your product. This step helps you identify points of friction, bottlenecks, and areas for improvement.

4.1.2 Clarity and Simplicity

Your prototype should be intuitive and easy to use. A clear and straightforward design eliminates user confusion and reduces the learning curve.

- **Simplicity**: Only include essential elements in your design. This approach makes it easy for users to find what they need.
- **Consistency**: Ensure the design elements, such as colors, fonts, and buttons, are consistent across your product.
- **Feedback**: Provide users with real-time feedback on their actions. This interaction helps them understand the system's current state and prevents errors.

4.1.3 Design Process and Tools

Developing a prototype is an iterative process. It usually starts with a first draft, followed by multiple design and feedback cycles before reaching the final version. There are many tools available for creating digital prototypes, such as Figma, Sketch, and Adobe XD. Choose the tool that best fits your needs and start exploring its features.

- **Sketching**: Start with a pen and paper to sketch out low-fidelity wireframes, also known as mockups. This step allows you to visualize your ideas and iterate quickly without getting bogged down by the tool's intricacies.
- **Wireframing**: Create more refined digital mockups, emphasizing the layout and structure of your design. This step further defines the user interface (UI) elements and their relationships.
- **High-Fidelity Prototyping**: Develop a high-fidelity, interactive prototype using your preferred design tool. The goal is to create a realistic representation of your final product, which can be tested with real users.

4.2 User Testing and Validation

Once you have designed your prototype, it's time to put it in front of real users to collect valuable insight into its usability, desirability, and feasibility.

4.2.1 Test Objectives and Participant Recruitment

Before conducting user tests, establish clear objectives to help evaluate the prototype's performance. Consider the following:

- Relevance - Test your value proposition and overall product concept.
- Usability - Assess the ease of use and learnability of your prototype.

- Desirability - Evaluate the emotional response and user satisfaction.

Once you know your testing goals, recruit participants who resemble your target users to ensure valid and actionable insights.

4.2.2 Types of User Testing

There are various user testing methods, ranging from informal to formal techniques. Choose the method that best suits your needs and resources.

- **Guerilla testing**: An informal, quick, and cost-effective method of testing that involves taking your prototype to public places and asking people for their feedback.
- **Remote usability testing**: Conduct tests online using tools like UsabilityHub or Lookback.io, enabling you to test with participants worldwide.
- **In-person usability testing**: Invite participants to your test location for a moderated testing session. This method allows for more in-depth, qualitative feedback.

4.2.3 Analyzing Results and Iterating

After collecting user feedback, the next step is to analyze the results and identify areas of improvement. Look for patterns and trends, such as recurring issues or positive aspects that can inform enhancement opportunities. Use this information to iterate on your prototype and refine your design.

Remember, the goal is to create a compelling user experience that resonates with your target audience. By following the principles of product design, empathizing with users, and testing rigorously, you can bring your no-code MVP to life and set the foundation for a successful startup.

4.1 Crafting the perfect prototype: Tips and tools for no-code MVPs

Before discussing various tips on product design and prototyping for your new no-code MVP, it is essential to first understand what a prototype is. A prototype is essentially an interactive simulation of your final product made with the sole purpose of testing and validating it. It enables you to identify key user experience friction points, potential technical limitations, and design flaws, which can be overcome before the launch.

Designing a compelling user experience starts with creating a well-crafted prototype. The objective of this subsection is to provide you with practical advice and introduce you to the best tools to help you in your journey to designing the perfect no-code MVP.

4.1.1 Define your goals and target audience

The first step in designing a compelling prototype is to clearly define the intent and goals of your product, as well as the target audience. This foundational work will ensure that your design process is in alignment with your overall product strategy.

Goals

- Outline your product objectives: These may include increasing user engagement, driving sales, or boosting brand awareness.

- Define your MVP (Minimum Viable Product): Figure out what minimal set of features can help you achieve the desired outcomes, while consuming the least possible resources.

Target Audience

- Who are your ideal customers/users? Be specific and create user personas that list demographics, behaviors, and preferences.
- Identify their pain points and needs, so you can tailor your solution to solving those problems.

4.1.2 Sketch your user flow and user interfaces

Your prototype should embody a visitor's journey through your product, and outline the steps they will take to achieve their desired outcome. Here's how to go about sketching these flows and interfaces:

- Create a high-level description of each user journey, breaking down the steps users will take, buttons clicked, and information they will need to complete their objectives.
- For each corresponding step, create a rough sketch of the user interface that includes the necessary elements for that interaction. Focus on simplicity and clarity in your sketches.

4.1.3 Choose your no-code product design and prototyping tools

With your sketches in hand, you will need a suite of tools to start the actual design process. There are many no-code tools available on the market that cater to various design capabilities and budgets. Here are some popular no-code design tools to help you create a professional-looking prototype:

- **Figma:** A cloud-based design tool that is easy to learn and comes with a robust free plan. Figma allows for real-time collaboration and supports the entire prototyping process, including design, wireframing, and prototyping.
- **Sketch:** A MacOS-specific design tool with a powerful interface and plugins that make it a popular choice among designers. Though not a no-code tool, it's essential to note that many other no-code tools integrate with Sketch.
- **Adobe XD:** A feature-rich tool with a user interface similar to other Adobe products. XD offers design, prototyping and collaboration tools, and design systems management, all within one application.

4.1.4 Test and iterate

Testing your prototype is an invaluable step towards identifying any potential issues and weaknesses in the design. Moreover, it will help you refine your solution and eventually create a better end product. To test and iterate effectively, consider the following:

- **User testing:** Conduct usability tests with your target audience, ideally using your user personas. Have them go through the various user journeys in your prototype and collect feedback.
- **Feedback:** Encourage users to provide honest feedback on their overall experience, as well as the aspects they enjoyed, didn't understand, or disliked. This information will provide actionable insights on what to improve.

- **Iteration:** Use the feedback gathered to update your prototype, implementing changes and improvements. This may involve tweaking the user interface or even revisiting your entire design strategy.

4.1.5 Always aim for improvement

Recognize that user experience is a moving target, and there will always be room for improvement. Embrace a culture of continuous learning, experimentation and iteration to ensure that your product never stops improving. Keep an eye on emerging design trends, innovation in technology, and user behavior changes to stay ahead in the game.

By following these practical steps and with the help of no-code tools, you can quickly build and validate a well-designed prototype for your startup idea. A compelling user experience will undoubtedly be the cornerstone of your product's success, so invest the time and effort to make your prototype engaging, visually appealing, and easy to use.

5. Building Your No-Code MVP: Step-by-Step Guide

5.2. Preparing and Planning for Your No-Code MVP

Before you start building your no-code MVP, it's essential to thoroughly prepare and plan your project to ensure that your MVP effectively validates your startup idea. Proper planning also helps you maximize the benefits of using no-code tools and minimizes any potential roadblocks during development.

Here, we will break down the planning process into smaller steps and dive into each of them.

5.2.1. Define Your Problem Statement

It all starts with identifying the problem you want to solve. Your problem statement should be concise, clear, and focused on the pain point you are addressing. Consider the following questions when crafting your problem statement:

- What is the problem you are trying to solve?
- Who is facing this problem?
- Why is this problem worth solving?

An effective problem statement should look something like this: "Freelance designers face difficulty managing their projects and communicating with clients, resulting in lost time and revenue."

5.2.2. Establish Your Target Market

Once you have identified the problem you want to solve, the next step is to pinpoint the target market that would benefit most from your solution. Conduct market research to identify your target demographic, understand their needs and preferences, and assess the profitability of your niche. A well-defined target market enables you to create a personalized user experience and increases the likelihood of your no-code MVP resonating with users.

5.2.3. Outline Your Value Proposition

Your value proposition sets you apart from competitors and highlights the unique benefits your solution offers your target market. It should sum up the key factors that make your product ideal for addressing the problem you've identified. Write a compelling value proposition to succinctly express your product's value and the reasons users should choose your solution over others.

5.2.4. Sketch Out Your User Flows

User flows are a visual representation of the steps users take to accomplish a specific action on your app or website. Start by identifying the most important actions you want users to perform in your no-code MVP, such as signing up, logging in, making a purchase, or providing feedback. Then, sketch out the paths users take to complete those actions. Mapping out user flows helps you create a seamless user experience and ensure your no-code MVP caters to your users' needs.

5.2.5. List the Features and Functionality

Now is the time to define the features and functionality you'll include in your no-code MVP. The key here is to prioritize the minimum set of features necessary to test your hypothesis and validate your idea. Choose the features that align with your problem statement and provide the most value to your users. Remember, your goal is to build a lean, testable prototype, so avoid over-engineering and stick to essentials.

5.2.6. Choose Your No-Code Tools and Platforms

With a clear understanding of what you want to build, it's time to choose the no-code tools that best fit your project requirements. You'll need to evaluate various no-code platforms regarding ease of use, integration capabilities, scalability, cost, and support options. Use your list of features and functionality, as well as your user flows, to guide your selection process. It's crucial to choose the right tools early on, as switching mid-development can be time-consuming and costly.

5.2.7. Develop a Testing and Feedback Plan

To ensure the success of your no-code MVP, it's crucial to gather user feedback and iterate on your product based on that input. Establish a solid testing and feedback framework that includes:

- Identifying the key performance indicators (KPIs) you'll use to evaluate your MVP.
- Deciding when and how to collect user feedback (e.g., surveys, interviews, analytics, or user testing).
- Integrating a feedback loop into your development process to inform future iterations and improvements.

5.2.8. Create a Timeline and Resource Plan

Finally, map out a project timeline that includes milestones and target completion dates for the various tasks and features. Allocate resources, such as your team members, to specific tasks based on their skills and expertise. Account for potential delays, such as tool limitations or unexpected development issues.

Completing these steps will equip you with a comprehensive plan to guide your no-code MVP creation. With your plan in hand, you can proceed with building, testing, and iterating on your product to quickly validate your startup idea and propel it towards success.

5.2 Defining Your MVP's Core Features

To create a successful no-code MVP (Minimum Viable Product), you need to define the core features of your product that will be built, tested, and delivered in the shortest possible time. These core features should be enough to solve the primary problem or satisfy the main need of your target customers, allowing you to validate your startup idea quickly and iteratively. In this section, we'll go through a step-by-step guide for defining your MVP's core features.

5.2.1 Establish Your Value Proposition

Start by identifying the main value proposition of your product or service. What is the primary problem or need that your product is addressing? What value will your customers get by using your product? Be as specific as possible while describing the value proposition because it will help you to focus on the essential features to deliver that value.

For example, let's consider a fictional no-code app – "BudgetBuddy." BudgetBuddy's value proposition is to help users actively manage and track their personal finances within a single platform, enabling them to make informed decisions about their spending habits to save more.

5.2.2 Determine Your Primary Users and Their Needs

Identify who you are building the MVP for and what their needs are. Your primary users may be a subset of your target audience, and their needs will help you prioritize which features to include in your MVP. Start by creating 2-3 detailed user personas that represent your primary users, and list down their specific needs related to your value proposition.

For BudgetBuddy, the primary users might be:

1. Young working professionals who typically overspend on non-essential items and want to save more by tracking their spending.
2. Freelancers who need to monitor their income and expenses to ensure they are earning more than they spend each month.

5.2.3 List Your Product's Feature Ideas

Brainstorm and make a comprehensive list of all the possible features that could be part of your product. This list should include anything that could be potentially useful or noteworthy for your users. Don't worry about prioritizing or filtering your ideas at this stage – the goal is to have an exhaustive list to choose from when defining your MVP's core features.

For our example, BudgetBuddy's feature ideas list could include:

1. Automatic expense tracking by connecting the user's bank account
2. Categorizing transactions into different expense categories
3. Customizable budgets for different spending categories
4. Visual charts to analyze spending habits
5. Bill reminders and notifications
6. Financial goal setting and tracking
7. Savings challenges and gamification
8. Expense splitting with friends or family members

5.2.4 Prioritize Features Based on Your Value Proposition and User Needs

Now that you have a list of possible features, it's time to prioritize them based on how well they align with your value proposition and your primary users' needs. For each feature, assess:

1. The importance of the feature in delivering the core value proposition
2. The level of complexity and time required to build the feature
3. The desirability of the feature by your primary users

For each feature, give a score based on these criteria, and use that score to determine which features should be considered for your MVP. Keep in mind that an MVP should focus on delivering the primary value to users as quickly and effectively as possible, so it's crucial to prioritize features that directly contribute to that value.

Continuing with the BudgetBuddy example, the following features might make it into the MVP version:

1. Automatic expense tracking by connecting the user's bank account
2. Categorizing transactions into different expense categories
3. Customizable budgets for different spending categories
4. Basic visual charts to analyze spending habits

These features directly address the users' needs and deliver the core value proposition while keeping the complexity and development time low.

5.2.5 Design Your MVP's User Flow & Wireframes

Once you've decided on the core features for your no-code MVP, you'll need to design the user flow and wireframes to visualize how users will interact with your product. Start by defining the main user journeys and then create wireframes for each step in the journey.

Using simple design tools like Balsamiq or Figma, create a visual representation of your MVP's user interface, including the layout, navigational elements, and interaction design. This will help ensure that your MVP is easy to use and feels intuitive for users, which is essential for its success.

5.2.6 Finalize Your MVP Scope and Begin Building

With the core features, user flows, and wireframes in place, you now have a clear understanding of what your no-code MVP will look and feel like when completed. This is the blueprint you will use to build your MVP using no-code tools like Webflow, Bubble, Adalo, or others, depending on your specific needs and requirements.

Remember, the primary goal of your no-code MVP is to validate your startup idea as quickly as possible. So, while building the MVP, focus on the core features and functionality rather than perfecting the design or polishing every aspect. You'll have plenty of time to iterate and improve upon the MVP once you've gathered valuable feedback and insights from real users.

In summary, defining your MVP's core features is a crucial step in building a successful no-code MVP. By focusing on delivering the primary value to your users as quickly and effectively as possible, you'll be one step closer to validating your startup idea and achieving your entrepreneurial goals.

5.1 Understanding Your Value Proposition

Before diving into the actual creation of your No-Code MVP, it is essential to understand and identify your product's value proposition. The value proposition is a significant aspect that defines the purpose of your product and the value it will provide to your target audience. It establishes the core challenges your product solves and differentiates it from existing competitors.

To define your value proposition, it is useful to follow these steps:

5.1.1 Identify and Understand Your Target Customers

Start by identifying who will be using your product. Answering the following questions may help you in defining your target audience:

1. What is their age group?
2. What defines their behavior?
3. What do they need?
4. How do they interact with technology?
5. What are their challenges and pain points?

Create detailed user personas that represent your target audience to gain a deeper understanding of their needs and preferences.

5.1.2 Determine Customer Needs and Problems

Once you have a clear understanding of your target audience, the next step involves identifying the specific challenges or pain points they face. You can do this by conducting surveys, interviews, or engaging in observation studies. Make a list of the most common customer problems, as they will become the foundation for your product's value proposition.

5.1.3 Identify Existing Solutions and Competitors

Evaluate the solutions available in the market that address your target customers' needs. It will give you an overview of the competition, and you can learn from their strengths and weaknesses. Make a list of your competitors and their value propositions to get a clearer picture of the competitive landscape.

5.1.4 Develop a Unique and Compelling Value Proposition

Based on your understanding of customer needs and the competitive landscape, the next step is to develop a unique and compelling value proposition for your product. You should be able to articulate it in a single sentence, addressing the core problem you aim to solve and how your product is different from the competition.

Remember, your value proposition focuses on the most crucial problem that you intend to solve while differentiating your product from others.

5.2 Choosing the Right No-Code Tools

With a clear understanding of your value proposition, you can now focus on identifying the right no-code tools to build your MVP. No-code tools come in various shapes and sizes, each with its advantages and limitations.

Consider the following factors when selecting the right no-code tools:

1. Functionality: Ensure that the tools you select can cater to your specific requirements, including the necessary features and integrations.

2. Ease of use: Choose tools that are easy to learn and navigate, which will allow you to create your MVP faster.
3. Scalability: Some no-code tools give you more room to expand and grow your product; choose wisely to avoid roadblocks in the future.
4. Cost: Ensure that the tools fit within your budget, and account for any usage limits or hidden costs.

There is a wide range of no-code tools available in the market, such as:

- Webflow: A visual designer to build responsive websites and web applications
- Bubble: A platform for creating web applications with powerful logic
- Adalo: A mobile app builder for creating native Android and iOS apps
- Zapier: An automation tool to connect multiple services and create workflows
- Airtable: A spreadsheet-database hybrid platform for data management

5.3 Building Your MVP

Once you have your value proposition and your no-code tools selected, it's time to start building your MVP. Here is a step-by-step guide to create your No-Code MVP:

5.3.1 Define Your MVP Features

Begin by outlining the features your MVP must contain to address your users' primary need. Focus on keeping the feature set minimal to validate your value proposition as quickly as possible. Avoid overloading the MVP with unnecessary elements.

5.3.2 Sketch Your User Interface (UI)

Visually plan your MVP's user interface, creating sketches or wireframes that represent each screen or view. Use these sketches to establish the layout and flow of your MVP. Keep the design simple and easy to navigate for your users.

5.3.3 Build Your UI Using No-Code Tools

Leverage the selected no-code tools to recreate your wireframes and implement a user interface for your MVP based on your sketches. Ensure that the design is responsive and visually appealing, keeping in mind the target audience.

5.3.4 Implement Your MVP Features

Use the chosen no-code tools to implement your core features. Set up any necessary integrations and workflows to ensure the MVP works seamlessly. Test each function to ensure it accurately addresses the user's pain points.

5.4 Testing and Validating Your MVP

After completing your MVP, it's time to test and validate it with real users. Start by collecting user feedback, identifying any gaps or issues, and iterating on the MVP before launching it publicly. Leverage analytics tools to monitor user engagement and measure the success of your MVP.

Following these steps will enable you to create and validate your startup ideas quickly by leveraging the power of no-code tools. Embrace the concept of embracing, learning, and iterating to build successful products that address your target audience's needs.

5. Building Your No-Code MVP: Step-by-Step Guide

5.1 Identifying Your Value Proposition

Before diving into the process of building your no-code MVP, it's essential to clarify the value proposition of your startup idea. A value proposition is the unique combination of features, benefits, and pricing that makes your product or service attractive to potential customers. Take the time to understand your target audience, their needs, and how your product or service satisfies those needs better than your competitors. Make sure your value proposition is simple, clear, and easy to communicate.

To help you identify your value proposition, consider answering the following questions:

1. Who is your target audience?
2. What problem are you solving for them?
3. How does your solution address their needs better than alternatives?

5.2 Selecting the Right No-Code Tools

The beauty of building a no-code MVP is that there are numerous platforms and tools available to help you create your product, ranging from simple drag-and-drop website builders to more advanced tools tailored for specific platforms, such as e-commerce or mobile app development. When selecting the best no-code tools for your MVP, consider your startup's primary focus, the ease of use, the level of customization, and the cost of the solution.

Some popular no-code tools include:

1. Webflow: For building responsive websites without writing any code
2. Bubble: A powerful platform to create web apps with its visual builder and database capabilities
3. Glide: Transform Google Sheets into mobile apps without writing any code
4. Zapier: Automate workflows and integrate various apps without coding
5. Airtable: Create customizable databases and project management systems

5.3 Designing Your MVP

Now that you have a clear value proposition and the right no-code tools at hand, it's time to design your MVP. Good design is about more than just aesthetics; it's about providing a user experience that makes it easy and enjoyable for people to achieve their goals using your product. Focus on the main user flow and ensure that your MVP's design revolves around solving the core problem you've identified.

During the design phase, consider the following steps:

1. **Sketch out your ideas**: Start with pen and paper, or use digital tools like Miro or Figma to create wireframes and mock-ups of your MVP's key screens.

2. **Test your designs**: Share your mock-ups with potential users or peers to gather feedback on the user experience and make necessary improvements.
3. **Create a design system**: Establish color schemes, typefaces, and reusable components to maintain consistency throughout your MVP, making it easier for end-users to navigate.
4. **Iterate and refine**: Continuously refine your design based on ongoing feedback and testing to ensure a straightforward, engaging user experience.

5.4 Building the MVP

With your value proposition defined, no-code tools selected, and a solid design plan in place, it's time to build your no-code MVP. Follow these steps to create a functional version of your product:

1. *Set up the structure* - Use your no-code tool to define the structure of your MVP. This might include creating pages, forms, and other UI elements to align with your wireframes and mock-ups.
2. *Add functionality* - Implement features that deliver your MVP's core value proposition. Depending on your chosen no-code platform, this could involve connecting actions to buttons, setting up workflows, or integrating with other tools and services.
3. *Customize the design* - Apply your design system to your MVP, including colors, typography, and component styles, to bring it in line with your visual design plan.
4. *Configure integrations* - In many cases, your MVP might require connecting with other tools, such as email providers or payment gateways. Use platforms like Zapier or Integromat to establish these

connections and streamline your users' interactions with your product.

5.5 Testing & Iterating

Once your no-code MVP is built, it's crucial not to stop there. One of the main advantages of no-code development is the ability to quickly test your product and iterate based on user feedback. Testing your MVP ensures that it not only functions correctly but also solves the problem it intends to solve.

1. *Gather feedback* - Share your MVP with potential customers, peers, or mentors to collect feedback on its usability, functionality, and overall value.
2. *Measure performance* - Use analytics tools to track user actions, monitor engagement, and determine if your MVP is meeting its goals.
3. *Identify areas for improvement* - Based on feedback and measurements, pinpoint specific areas of your MVP that need improvement, such as design, content, or user flow.
4. *Make adjustments* - Use your no-code tools to make changes to your MVP based on your findings, ensuring you're continuously refining your product based on user needs and feedback.
5. *Repeat the process* - The testing and iterating process is ongoing, as your product continues to evolve based on user input and other external factors.

By following this step-by-step guide for building your no-code MVP, you'll be well-equipped to quickly and efficiently validate your startup idea without the need for extensive programming experience or a large development team. Keep iterating and refining your product, staying focused on your value proposition, and maintaining flexibility to adapt based on valuable user feedback.

5.1 Define the Problem and Form Hypotheses

Before diving into building your no-code MVP, it's essential to start by defining the problem you are trying to solve and formulating the assumptions about why your solution will add value to the market. This initial stage will help you focus on the right features and functionality when designing and building your MVP.

5.1.1 Define the Problem

Begin by stating the problem your startup idea aims to solve in clear and concise language. Think through the pain points that your target customers are experiencing and make sure your problem statement addresses them. A well-defined problem statement will help you stay focused on creating the most important features for your no-code MVP.

5.1.2 Identify Target Customers

Next, identify who your target customers are. Consider creating personas to represent the types of people who will benefit from your solution. Describe their demographics, needs, behaviors, and preferences. Understanding your target customers deepens your understanding of the problem and helps you develop a solution that addresses their needs.

5.1.3 Formulate Hypotheses

With a clear problem statement and understanding of your target customer, it's time to start defining the assumptions you need to test. Formulate a set of hypotheses about how your product will solve the identified problem, improve user experience, and add value to the market.

Your main hypothesis should directly link your solution to the problem. Additional hypotheses may cover features you believe will be crucial for customer satisfaction, engagement, and retention.

For example, if your problem statement is "Freelancers struggle to manage their finances effectively," your main hypothesis might be "A mobile app that simplifies financial management for freelancers will help them save time and make smarter financial decisions."

5.2 Design and Build Your No-Code MVP

Once you have defined the problem and formed hypotheses, it's time to move on to designing and building your no-code MVP. Focus on testing the most critical assumptions and creating only the essential features using no-code tools.

5.2.1 Decide on a No-Code Platform

Choose a no-code platform that best fits your needs and skillset. There are various no-code platforms available, including web app builders (e.g., Bubble, Webflow), mobile app builders (e.g., Adalo, Glide), and functional tools (e.g., Zapier, Airtable). Consider the following factors when choosing a no-code platform:

- Does it have the features you need for your MVP?
- Is it easy to use and learn?

- Can it scale and support more advanced features in future iterations?
- Does it fit your budget?

5.2.2 Prototype and Test Essential Features

Start by building the must-have features to test your main hypothesis. This may include user registration, basic UI elements for navigation, and core functionality for problem-solving.

Build your no-code MVP by following the platform's guidelines and tutorials. Keep your target customers in mind when designing the interface and make the user experience as smooth as possible. Consider using pre-built templates provided by the no-code platform or design tools like Figma to save time.

Remember, your goal is to test the viability of your startup idea, so avoid adding unnecessary features or making the MVP too polished.

5.2.3 Test, Evaluate, and Compare Alternatives

After building the essential features, test your MVP internally first to ensure it works as intended. Gather feedback from colleagues or friends who fit your target customer profile. Fix any bugs and improve the UX based on this feedback.

Next, identify alternative solutions in the market that your target customers might already be using. Evaluate your no-code MVP against these alternatives to understand where your solution excels and where it falls short. This comparison will also help you better understand your unique value proposition and competition.

5.3 Collect Feedback and Iterate

Now that your no-code MVP is ready and tested, collect feedback from real users to validate your assumptions and make data-driven improvements to the product.

5.3.1 Launch MVP and Monitor Metrics

Deploy your no-code MVP on a domain or app store and promote it to your target customers. Collect relevant metrics, such as user sign-ups, feature usage, and retention rates, to measure success and evaluate your hypotheses.

5.3.2 Collect User Feedback

Gather feedback directly from your users to understand what they like and dislike about your MVP. Reach out through surveys or interviews to gain additional insights into how your product is solving—or failing to solve—the problem for your target customers.

5.3.3 Iterate and Optimize

Analyze the gathered metrics and feedback to determine whether your hypotheses are validated or refuted. Use these insights to iterate on your product, making improvements and adding or removing features as necessary.

Remember that building a successful startup is an iterative process, so continue refining your no-code MVP by collecting user feedback, testing new features, and adjusting your hypotheses until you reach product-market fit.

6. Testing and Validating Your MVP: User Feedback and Analytics

6.1 Obtaining and Evaluating User Feedback

The most critical aspect of your Minimum Viable Product (MVP) is determining its relevance and value proposition to your target audience. This requires a continuous process of testing, evaluating, and iterating based on user feedback and analytics.

User feedback is invaluable in helping you understand how your product works for real users. It not only helps you identify issues and bottlenecks in the MVP but also helps you identify areas that need improvement or features that users would like to see. Feedback can come from various sources, including one-on-one interviews, focus groups, online surveys, and in-app rating systems. Regardless of the method you choose, it's crucial to approach this process systematically and thoughtfully.

6.1.1 Identifying Your Target Audience

Before gathering feedback, you must determine who your audience is. Having a clear understanding of who will use your product and the problems it solves will help you create an MVP that aligns with user needs.

- **Market segmentation**: Break down your target market into smaller segments based on factors like demographics, geography, and behavioral patterns. This will help you better understand the needs and preferences of various groups and design your product to cater to their specific needs.

- **Identifying personas**: Personas are fictional representations of typical users within a segment, consisting of their goals, challenges, preferences, and motivations. Developing personas can provide a foundation for determining the specific user groups you wish to target and evaluate your MVP.
- **Conducting user interviews**: Conduct interviews with prospective users to understand their motivations, pain points, and current solutions to the problems your MVP aims to address. Use these insights to target the right user segments and design an MVP tailored to their needs.

6.1.2 Collecting Feedback

Once you've identified your target audience, you need to choose the appropriate methods for collecting feedback. There is no one-size-fits-all solution, and you may need to use a combination of methods to get a comprehensive understanding of user experiences.

- **In-person or remote interviews**: One-on-one interviews are an efficient way to gain deep insights into a user's thought process and experience with your MVP. You can observe how they interact with your product, ask questions, and delve deeper into their feedback. Remote interviews may be conducted via video conferencing tools if in-person meetings aren't attainable.
- **Focus groups**: A focus group involves gathering a small group of people representing your target audience and facilitating discussions about your MVP. Focus groups can help gauge overall sentiment,

capture group dynamics, and uncover areas of improvement.

- **Online surveys**: Surveys offer a quick and cost-effective way to gather feedback from many users simultaneously. Create well-designed questionnaires, analyze the qualitative and quantitative data, and use these insights to refine your MVP.
- **Social media monitoring**: Monitor social media platforms for user-generated feedback, comments, and reviews about your MVP. This can provide valuable information about user sentiment and potential areas for improvement.

6.1.3 Analyzing User Feedback

Simply collecting feedback is not enough; you must also analyze it systematically to ensure that you can apply the insights gained into improving your MVP.

- **Categorize feedback**: Organize the feedback received into different categories like usability, features, design, and performance. Categorizing feedback will help you identify patterns and areas that require your attention and prioritize tasks for the next iteration of your MVP.
- **Quantitative analysis**: Analyze quantitative data, such as survey responses and app ratings, to gauge user sentiment and identify trends over time. Use tools like spreadsheets or specialized analytics software to analyze the data and generate actionable insights.
- **Qualitative analysis**: Analyze qualitative inputs, such as open-ended survey responses and interview transcripts, to uncover unique insights and individual user perspectives. Use coding techniques to identify recurring themes and patterns across the data to gain

a better understanding of users' experiences and expectations.

- **Visualization**: Create visual representations of your data analysis, such as charts, graphs, or heatmaps, to better understand the patterns and trends within the feedback.

6.1.4 Reacting to Feedback

Once you've analyzed the user feedback, the next step is to react and adapt. Use the insights from the feedback to improve your MVP and prepare it for the next testing phase.

- **Iterate**: Update your MVP using the feedback gathered, address user pain points, and add or refine features based on user demand. It's essential to maintain the lean nature of your product during this process and keep its core intact.
- **Regular updates**: Ensure users are aware of the changes you've made in response to their feedback. This transparency will help you build trust with your users and retain their attention and engagement.
- **Re-test**: After implementing the changes, re-test the improved version of your MVP with users to gather more feedback and refine it further. Continuously iterate and improve your MVP based on user feedback until it becomes a complete product that caters to users' needs and expectations.

Remember, the key to successful testing and validation of your MVP is to continuously adapt and improve based on user feedback and analytics. Obtain user feedback from a diverse range of sources, analyze the data collected, and apply these insights to make your MVP better. By following these steps, you can ensure that your MVP caters to real user needs and addresses genuine pain points, leading to a successful product launch.

6.2 The Importance of Gathering User Feedback and Analytics

Throughout the development and launch of your no-code MVP, you can easily become trapped in the mindset of 'if I just add this one more feature, it'll be perfect.' While the desire to create a perfect product is understandable, it often leads entrepreneurs to miss a crucial step in building a successful digital product – seeking out and acting upon user feedback and analytics.

User feedback and analytics are an essential part of the development process, as they offer insights into how your customers truly interact with, and perceive, your product. These insights are fundamental to maximizing the utility and value of your MVP, as they lead to informed decisions that impact product development, marketing, sales, and customer support.

In this section, we'll discuss various methods and tools for gathering user feedback and analytics, as well as how to interpret and act upon the insights gathered.

1. Utilize Feedback Channels

When it comes to getting user feedback, it's essential to give your customers various channels through which they can voice their opinions. These channels can include:

- **Customer Support:** Ensure that your support team is actively listening for customer feedback while addressing needs through email, live chat, or phone conversations. Instruct them to document any feedback for review and analysis.

- **Online Surveys:** Tools like Google Forms, SurveyMonkey, or Typeform allow you to create comprehensive surveys that can be sent to your customers. You can use these platforms to ask users direct questions about your product, gauge satisfaction levels, and to solicit general feedback.
- **Social Media:** Monitor your social media accounts for any feedback that may come through direct messages or comments on your posts. Encourage users to provide their opinions by actively engaging with them and addressing any concerns.
- **User Feedback Forms:** Embed user feedback forms on your website or within your MVP, allowing users to easily provide feedback at any time during their experience with your product.

2. In-App Analytics

In addition to gathering qualitative data from users, you must consider collecting quantitative data using analytics tools. These tools monitor user behavior and can provide invaluable insights for making data-driven improvements to your product. Examples of analytics tools include:

- **Google Analytics:** A popular and powerful analytics tool that can offer insights about how users are engaging with your website, including metrics like session durations, bounce rates, and user flow. You can also set up conversion-tracking goals to measure how effectively your MVP is meeting business objectives.
- **Mixpanel:** Mixpanel is an event-based analytics platform that tracks user interactions with your

product in real-time. It provides granular insights into how users engage with different features or functionalities, revealing patterns that can lead to optimization opportunities.

- **Amplitude:** Similar to Mixpanel, Amplitude is another platform that enables you to analyze customer behavior data at scale. With a focus on growth, you can use Amplitude's data to optimize user retention, improve onboarding experiences, and personalize customer engagements.

3. Analyzing the Data

Simply gathering user feedback and analytics isn't enough; you must take the time to thoroughly review and interpret the data, looking for patterns and trends that may suggest opportunities for improvement. Consider the following steps in your data analysis process:

1. **Organize User Feedback:** Categorize feedback and use a system to prioritize the most urgent or impactful insights for immediate action.
2. **Identify Common Themes:** Look for repeating issues, requests, or concerns across multiple user comments, as these may represent areas that need immediate improvement.
3. **Track Metrics and KPIs:** Using tools like dashboards, track key performance indicators (KPIs) and other essential metrics in order to monitor progress and make data-driven decisions.
4. **Create Action Plans:** Based on the analysis of collected feedback, develop action plans addressing critical issues, and determine how these plans can be implemented and monitored for success.
5. **Continuously Iterate:** The process of gathering, analyzing, and acting upon user feedback should be

never-ending. Continuously improve your product with user feedback and analytics, staying true to the agile and adaptive mindset that inspired your no-code MVP in the first place.

In Conclusion

Your no-code MVP is a means to gather valuable user feedback and insights, which can inform decisions and facilitate growth. Through proactive gathering and thoughtful analysis of both qualitative and quantitative data, you can create a product that resonates with your target audience and evolves to meet their needs. Embrace the iterative nature of the MVP process, and let user feedback and analytics be your compass on the journey to creating a successful digital product.

6. Testing and Validating Your MVP: User Feedback and Analytics

An MVP, or a Minimum Viable Product, is a prototype of your product that includes just enough features to validate its core value. By testing and validating your no-code MVP, you can save considerable amounts of time and resources that are otherwise spent developing features users might not find valuable.

In this section, we will discuss the essential aspects of testing and validating your no-code MVP. We will cover strategies for gathering user feedback, analyzing usage data and analytics, and iterating on your MVP for increased market fit.

6.1. Preparing for User Feedback

User feedback is crucial to understand if your MVP provides the expected value to your target audience. To gather insights from real users, you need to prepare a well-structured feedback process. Here are some essential steps to follow:

6.1.1. Define Your Target Audience

The first and most crucial step in obtaining valuable feedback is identifying your target audience. Be specific about demographics, interests, and behaviors that describe your ideal users. By defining your target audience, you can confidently explore the right channels to reach potential users and request their feedback.

6.1.2. Create a User Feedback Plan

Create a plan that identifies how you will collect user feedback, who will be responsible for collecting and analyzing it, how much feedback you aim to collect, and the timeline for feedback collection. This plan will help you in staying organized and focused during your MVP testing phase.

6.1.3. Develop a User-friendly Feedback Channel

Develop an easy and accessible way for users to share their thoughts on your MVP. This can be a simple online form, an email address, or even direct messages on social media platforms. Make sure to communicate that you appreciate and value their input.

6.2. Gathering User Feedback

Once you're well-prepared and know who to target, it's time to gather the user feedback. Here are some methods to reach your target audience and collect their thoughts:

6.2.1. Surveys and Questionnaires

Create concise and well-structured surveys or questionnaires to collect quantitative data from your target audience. There are numerous online tools like Google Forms, SurveyMonkey, or Typeform to create and distribute your survey. Use a mix of open-ended and close-ended questions to capture detailed responses.

6.2.2. Interviews

Conducting one-on-one interviews with users offers deeper insights into their experience with your MVP. Prepare a set of questions related to your product, its features, and usability. Use open-ended questions like *"What did you like the most about this product?"* or *"What can be improved in this product?"* to get detailed and actionable feedback.

6.2.3. User Testing

Invite users to test your MVP in a controlled environment, either remotely or in person. Observe their interactions with your product, ask them to think aloud as they navigate through the features, and capture their natural reactions. This hands-on approach to user feedback is invaluable in understanding your MVP's usability and user experience.

6.3. Analyzing User Feedback and Analytics

After you gather user feedback, it's time to analyze the data and identify patterns that can guide your product iterations.

Here are some tips to help you analyze user feedback effectively:

6.3.1. Categorize Feedback

Categorize the user feedback by theme (e.g., usability, features, design) and priority (e.g., critical issues, improvements, nice-to-have). This will help you identify common pain points and areas of improvement.

6.3.2. Quantitative and Qualitative Analysis

Analyze quantitative data (e.g., survey results) to understand the overall user sentiment and identify trends. Analyze qualitative feedback (e.g., interview responses) to gain deeper insights into users' thoughts and perceptions. Combining both quantitative and qualitative data will provide a holistic understanding of your MVP's performance.

6.3.3. Use No-code Analytics Tools

No-code analytics tools, such as Google Analytics, Hotjar, or Mixpanel, can provide valuable insights into how users interact with your MVP. These tools can help you track user activity, identify any bottlenecks, and measure the overall user experience.

6.4. Iterating and Monitoring

Using the insights from user feedback and analytics, it's time to iterate on your product and improve its functionality, usability, or appearance. Continuously monitor user feedback, track your KPIs, and make data-driven decisions to improve your MVP.

In conclusion, testing and validating your no-code MVP is a crucial step towards building a successful product. By gathering user feedback, analyzing usage data, and iterating based on user insights, you can significantly increase the chances of your product resonating with your target audience and achieving success in the market.

6.1 Importance of User Feedback and Analytics in No-Code MVP

Before we dive into the methods and tools that you can use to test and validate your no-code MVP, let us understand why user feedback and analytics are necessary in the first place. Building a startup from scratch is a resource-consuming and time-intensive process. You do not want to waste your efforts in building a product that nobody needs or wants. This is where the validation of your MVP comes into the picture.

An MVP (Minimum Viable Product) is a stripped-down version of your final product, developed to test market demand and ensure that you are on the right track. User feedback and analytics during the MVP stage can provide insights and information related to:

1. **Market demand:** Is there sufficient demand for your product?
2. **Value proposition:** Does your product solve a problem or fulfill a need for your target users?
3. **Usability:** Is your product easy to use and understand for your target audience?
4. **Feature prioritization:** Which features are considered essential by your users, and which ones can be added later or improved upon based on user feedback?

5. **Refinement and iteration:** How can you iterate and improve your MVP based on user feedback and analytical data?

To gather user feedback and analyze their behavior while using your no-code MVP, a combination of qualitative and quantitative methods are crucial.

Qualitative User Feedback

Qualitative feedback refers to any non-metric data that helps you understand how your users feel and perceive your MVP. Qualitative methods can include:

1. **User interviews:** Conduct interviews with early users of your MVP, focusing on understanding their overall experience, likes, dislikes, and areas of improvement that they suggest. It is essential to ask open-ended questions so as not to bias users' feedback.
2. **Focus groups:** Engage small groups of your target audience and ask them to provide feedback on your MVP in a discussion context. Focus groups can provide diverse opinions and lead to valuable debates about your product's features and value.
3. **User surveys and questionnaires:** Create detailed surveys and questionnaires, asking users about their experience, pain points, or improvements they visualize for the MVP. Surveys can also include open-ended feedback sections for more qualitative insights.
4. **Observation and task analysis:** Shadow users while they interact with your MVP, either in person or via screen-sharing tools. You can gain valuable first-hand insights into how users use your product, what aspects they find confusing or unintuitive, and what areas they tend to focus on most.

Quantitative User Analytics

Quantitative analytics refers to the numerical data collected on user behavior, which can be analyzed to gain insights into how users interact with your MVP. Several no-code tools allow you to track various user interactions in your product. Analytics data can help validate your hypotheses, uncover unexpected behavioral patterns, and help optimize your no-code MVP. Some quantitative methods to consider include:

1. **Usage metrics:** Gather analytics on the most-used features, the average time spent on your MVP, and the number of unique users visiting your site.
2. **Acquisition metrics:** Identify the most effective channels through which you acquire new users and measure the return on investment (ROI) for these channels.
3. **Retention and churn:** Measure user retention over time to understand if users continue to use your MVP and find it valuable or if they abandon it after the first few interactions.
4. **Conversion rates:** Track the conversion rates for various actions such as user signups, purchases, or other desired actions, depending on your MVP's goals.

Popular No-Code Analytics Tools

Here are some popular no-code analytics tools that you can quickly implement on your MVP:

1. Google Analytics: A powerful and widely used analytics tool to track user behavior and traffic sources.
2. Heap: An event-based analytics tool that automatically tracks user interactions like clicks and

page views, enabling you to analyze user behavior retroactively.

3. Mixpanel: A robust analytics tool that provides user behavior insights through funnel analysis, cohort analysis, and segmentation.
4. Hotjar: A user feedback and behavior analytics tool that provides heatmaps, session recordings, and user surveys.

As you progress in testing and validating your no-code MVP, having a good mix of qualitative and quantitative methods goes a long way in deriving actionable insights that can lead to better decision-making, feature prioritization, and user experience optimization. Always remember that the primary purpose of your MVP is to learn and iterate, so embrace feedback and analytics to ensure that you develop a product that delights your users and serves their needs effectively.

6.1 Gathering Essential User Feedback and Analyzing Data for Your No-Code MVP

Gaining insights from your users and analyzing the data collected during MVP testing is crucial for shaping and refining your product. This phase enables you to discard features that users find unappealing, confusing or unnecessary, and work on the ones that actually create value. In this section, we will outline various methods for gathering user feedback, and also discuss tools and strategies to make data-driven decisions for your no-code MVP.

6.1.1 User Surveys and Interviews

User Surveys: Surveys are a popular way of gathering feedback from users, as they are easy to create, disseminate, and can be made anonymous to encourage candid responses. Using survey tools such as Typeform, Survey Monkey, or even Google Forms, you can create your own surveys tailored to your MVP.

- Start with basic demographic questions (e.g., age, gender, location) to understand the profile of your users.
- Include questions about the user's experience with your MVP, such as how frequently they use it and what they like or dislike about it.
- Get specific feedback on individual features, as well as the overall usability of your product.
- Finally, ask open-ended questions to give users the opportunity to voice their opinions and provide suggestions.

Remember to keep the survey short and to the point to ensure a higher response rate.

User Interviews: While surveys can provide you with a great deal of information, a one-on-one conversation may sometimes be necessary to gain deeper insights. Schedule interviews with your users and ask them detailed questions about their experience with your product. During these discussions, observe the user's body language, tone, and word choice to better understand their emotions and reactions to your product.

6.1.2 In-app Feedback and Usability Testing

In-app Feedback Tools: It's important to make it as easy as possible for users to give feedback while they are engaged with your product. Integrating tools like UserReport, Hotjar, or Mopinion lets users submit suggestions, report bugs and express their opinions without leaving the app.

Usability Testing: This method involves observing users as they interact with your product, enabling you to identify any roadblocks or areas where they might struggle. You can run usability tests remotely using platforms such as UserTesting or TryMyUI or conduct them in person to get an up-close view of the user's experience.

6.1.3 Metrics and Data Analysis

Collecting metrics and analyzing data is crucial to measure the success of your MVP and make evidence-based decisions about its future development. While qualitative data like user feedback is essential, you should also use quantitative data to back up the insights you gather. Here are some key metrics to focus on:

- **Retention**: This indicates the number of users who continue using your product over time. High retention suggests that your MVP is providing value to users, while low retention highlights that there is room for improvement.
- **User acquisition**: The number of new users you acquire over a specific period signifies your growth. Compare your user acquisition rate with your retention rate to judge the overall success of your product.
- **Conversion rate**: If your MVP has an end goal (e.g., purchase, subscription, or registration), the conversion rate measures the percentage of users who complete that goal.
- **Engagement**: This encompasses various metrics like time spent on your app, frequency of use, and interactions with specific features. Engagement can

hint at the user satisfaction level and areas where improvement is needed.

6.1.4 Analyzing and Learning from the Data

It is not enough to simply gather feedback and data – you must analyze it and derive valuable insights that lead to action. Here are some best practices for analyzing and learning from the data:

- Look for patterns in user feedback, and prioritize the most commonly reported issues or suggestions for improvement.
- Analyze survey results using visual aids such as charts and graphs to easily identify trends and outliers.
- Establish a "feedback loop" by regularly reviewing and implementing changes based on user suggestions and tracking the outcome. This will help you iterate and improve your product over time.

By carefully evaluating your user feedback and analyzing the data from your MVP, you can identify areas of improvement, validate your initial assumptions, and better understand your target audience. Armed with this knowledge, you can make data-driven decisions to shape the future of your product, and ultimately determine the success of your startup idea.

7. Making Data-Driven Improvements: Refining and Optimizing Your Product

7.1. Collect Valuable User Data

The first step to making data-driven improvements to your no-code MVP is collecting valuable user data. The data you gather will allow you to understand how users are interacting with your product and reveal areas that need optimization.

7.1.1. Set Goals and KPIs

Before you start collecting data, it's crucial to identify your goals and key performance indicators (KPIs). These objectives should align with your overall business goals and should be specific, measurable, achievable, relevant, and time-bound (SMART).

Some common KPIs for no-code MVPs include:

- User engagement (time spent on the platform, pages visited, etc.)
- User acquisition (number of signups, conversion rate from visitor to customer, etc.)
- Retention (percentage of users who continue using the product after signup, etc.)

7.1.2. Establish Tracking Methods

Once you have defined your goals and KPIs, it's time to set up mechanisms to track user data. No-code MVPs benefit from various tools and platforms that enable you to monitor user interactions without writing a single line of code. Some popular analytics tools include Google Analytics, Mixpanel, and Amplitude.

To begin, identify the critical user flows in your product that align with your goals and KPIs. For example, if user acquisition is a primary goal, monitoring the user signup process should be a priority. Next, start implementing event tracking with your chosen analytics tool, ensuring you cover all relevant user actions within the target flows.

7.1.3. Segment and Analyze Data

After setting up tracking, you'll begin accumulating user data. The key is to analyze and interpret the data in a way that provides actionable insights. One effective method to achieve this is by segmenting your data based on user properties or actions.

For example, you may want to segment users by their traffic source to understand which marketing channels drive the most engaged users. Alternatively, you could segment users based on their in-app actions – such as those who completed a specific task or achieved a specific milestone.

By segmenting your data, you will uncover valuable insights into user behavior patterns and preferences, which can inform your MVP optimization efforts.

7.2. Prioritizing Product Improvements

With all the valuable insights you've gained from the data analysis, it's time to start making targeted product improvements. It's crucial to prioritize these improvements based on factors such as their potential impact, ease of implementation, and alignment with your goals and KPIs.

7.2.1. Create a Product Roadmap

Developing a product roadmap helps you plan and prioritize your improvements over a specific timeline. A simple yet effective method for creating a roadmap is using the ICE scoring framework, which stands for Impact, Confidence, and Ease.

- Impact: How much of an effect will this improvement have on your KPIs or business goals?
- Confidence: How sure you are that the improvement will have the expected outcome?
- Ease: How easy or challenging it is to implement the improvement?

Assign a score to each improvement idea based on these factors, and then calculate an overall score by averaging the category scores. This overall ICE score will help you prioritize improvements and determine which ones to tackle first.

7.2.2. Test and Iterate

After prioritizing your improvements, begin implementing them in your no-code MVP while monitoring the impact on your KPIs. Keep in mind that not all improvements will result in an instant change; some may take time to show noticeable results.

Embrace the process of continuous iteration and refinement as you analyze the impact of your changes and adjust your product roadmap accordingly. Run A/B tests to experiment with different solutions to find the most effective one for your target audience.

Remember that optimizing and refining your no-code MVP is a learning process that involves both successes and failures. Use your data-driven insights to make informed decisions and adapt to the ever-changing needs and preferences of your user base.

7.3. Foster a Data-Driven Culture

Data-driven improvements should not be a one-time exercise but rather be part of an ongoing commitment to continuous growth and improvement. Cultivating a data-driven mindset among your team members can help instill this practice throughout your organization.

7.3.1. Encourage Data Literacy

Ensure that everyone on your team understands the importance of data, the tools used for gathering and analyzing data, and how data-driven insights can inform product decisions. Empower team members by providing training and resources to improve their data literacy.

7.3.2. Share Progress and Successes

Regularly share data insights, progress updates, and success stories with your team. This promotes a culture of transparency and demonstrates the value of data-driven decision-making.

By following these steps and staying committed to making data-driven improvements, you'll be well-equipped to optimize and refine your no-code MVP. As a result, you'll create a product that better resonates with your target audience, setting your startup on a path to long-term success.

7.1 Analyzing User Feedback and Product Metrics to Optimize Your No-Code MVP

One of the key elements in the success of any startup is the ability to continue refining and optimizing the product based on data and user feedback. In this era of highly competitive and rapidly evolving markets, being able to pivot quickly and adapt is a cornerstone of success. When building a No-Code MVP, the goal should not only be to develop and launch your product, but also to utilize the power of data to make informed improvements, creating a more valuable and engaging product for your users. Here we will discuss how you can analyze user feedback and product metrics, enabling data-driven improvements for your No-Code MVP.

Data Collection

Before we dive into analyzing data and user feedback, we must first ensure that the right data points are being collected. The following are some essential aspects of data collection for a No-Code MVP:

1. **User behavior tracking**: Utilize analytics tools (such as Google Analytics or Mixpanel) to track user interaction with your product. Identify the key performance indicators (KPIs) of your application, and make sure your analytics tools are capable of tracking each KPI.
2. **Feature-usage reports**: Analyze how frequently each feature of your product is being used by your users. This information will give you an overview of which features are essential and used most often, and which

ones might require further improvement or reevaluation.
3. **User feedback**: Actively seek user feedback through various channels. You can utilize surveys, feedback widgets, social media, or direct contact with users to learn about their opinions on your product. Gathering qualitative data from user feedback helps you identify potential areas of improvement that might not be visible through purely quantitative product data.

Analyzing Quantitative Data and Identifying Trends

Once you have collected the relevant data, you should examine any emerging trends or patterns in your product's performance. Focus on your KPIs and other important metrics in this step. Perform the following analysis:

1. **Funnel analysis**: Understand the user journey and identify where potential bottlenecks are that might be causing drop-offs. For example, if users abandon your website during the sign-up process, you might need to simplify your registration form, or offer social login options.
2. **Cohort analysis**: Group users based on similar characteristics, such as when they joined, and compare their behaviors to identify trends. For example, you might find that users who discovered your product through a specific marketing channel have better retention rates.
3. **A/B Testing**: Experiment with different product features and changes to see what impact it has on user behavior. For example, you could test different color schemes or UI elements to understand which

version provides the best user experience for your target audience.

4. **Segmentation**: Analyze how different groups of users interact with your product to uncover valuable insights regarding your target audience. You may find that a certain group of users are more engaged than others, or have higher conversion rates.

Utilizing Qualitative Feedback to Inform Product Decisions

While quantitative data provides valuable insights, it is equally important to gather qualitative feedback from user experiences. Here are some ways to analyze qualitative user feedback effectively:

1. **Categorize feedback**: Identify recurring themes and pain points from user feedback. Categorize them into different areas such as improvements, feature requests, or bug reports.
2. **Prioritize user feedback**: Assess the impact and effort required to implement the feedback, and prioritize it accordingly. Focus on high-impact, low-effort improvements to maximize the value of the changes you make to your product.
3. **Detect user personas**: By analyzing user feedback, you can identify different user personas and their specific needs, allowing you to tailor your product to better serve those individual needs.

Implementing Data-Driven Improvements

Once you have conducted an in-depth analysis of both quantitative data and qualitative feedback, it is time to make data-driven improvements to your No-Code MVP. Follow these steps to ensure the success of your product refinement process:

1. **Create a development roadmap**: Detail and prioritize the improvements identified from your data analysis, and create a timeline for implementation.
2. **Communicate with users**: Inform your users of upcoming improvements and thank them for their valuable feedback. Highlight the changes that are a direct result of their input, to demonstrate that you value their opinions and are actively working to improve their experience.
3. **Iterate**: Continue to collect data and feedback even after implementing improvements. Analyze the outcome of your changes and continue refining your product based on user input.

By consistently analyzing user feedback and product metrics, you will be able to continually refine your No-Code MVP, resulting in a more successful product with greater user satisfaction. Remember, the key to achieving long-term success with your startup is an unrelenting focus on data-driven improvements, tailored to the evolving needs and desires of your users.

7.2 Conducting Quantitative Analysis: Find Key Metrics You Should Track

As you start to engage customers with your no-code MVP, it's vital to measure their behavior and interactions with your product. But before you start drowning in data, it's essential to determine the key metrics to track. By analyzing this data, you will uncover insights that help you make data-driven decisions, refine your MVP, and optimize its performance. In this section, we will explore how to perform quantitative analysis by identifying the key metrics, tracking them, and interpreting the findings.

7.2.1 Defining the Metrics That Matter

Depending on your product, industry, and target audience, the metrics you need to pay attention to might differ. However, there are some universal metrics that most startups find useful. These include:

1. **Acquisition**: Understanding where your users come from and which channels are the most effective in driving traffic to your MVP.
2. **Activation**: Measuring the percentage of acquired users who take the first valuable action, such as signing up, on your MVP.
3. **Retention**: Analyzing the rate at which users continue using your product after activation.
4. **Revenue**: Calculating the amount of money generated by your MVP.
5. **Referral**: Tracking users who promote your product by referring it to others.

These five metrics, also known as AARRR, are the Pirate Metrics developed by Dave McClure, founder of 500 Startups. Of course, these high-level metrics can be further broken down into specific actions or events that give you deeper insights. It's crucial to identify these specific metrics and track them regularly for meaningful quantitative analysis.

7.2.2 Tracking Your Metrics

Once you have identified the key metrics, you need tools to track them. Thanks to no-code platforms, you can easily integrate analytics without the need for coding or technical expertise. Some popular and accessible tools include:

- Google Analytics: A comprehensive analytics tool that tracks website traffic, user engagement, and other essential metrics.
- Mixpanel: A powerful analytics platform for mobile and web products, focused on tracking user actions (events) and segmenting users (cohorts).
- Hotjar: A tool that provides heatmaps, visitor recordings, and conversion funnels to help you optimize the user experience.

With the proper setup and configuration of these tools, you'll begin to collect valuable data that helps you understand how users are interacting with your MVP. Be sure to track user behavior from the very beginning, as this data will prove invaluable as you iterate on your MVP and optimize it for the best performance.

7.2.3 Interpreting and Acting on the Data

As you collect and analyze data from your MVP, you'll uncover insights that can help you address your customers' needs better. Look for trends, patterns, and anomalies in the data that might indicate opportunities for improvement or further investigation.

For example, if you notice that users frequently drop off at a specific point in your onboarding process, you may need to adjust the flow or provide more assistance during that step. Alternatively, if a marketing channel is driving a significant amount of traffic, it might be worth investing more resources in that channel to amplify its performance.

Remember, the goal is not to chase vanity metrics, but to identify opportunities and optimize your MVP to deliver the most value to your customers. As you come across new findings, it's important to keep testing and refining your product continuously.

7.2.4 Iterating and Experimenting

Your MVP must be flexible and adaptable to the constantly changing market demands and customer expectations. The traditional method of making substantial updates or product changes every six to twelve months will not suffice in today's fast-paced digital landscape.

Instead, adopt a mentality of rapid iteration and experimentation. Leverage the data you've collected and the insights you've gathered to continuously refine your MVP. Use A/B testing to compare different versions of your product or elements within it to determine which ones resonate the most with your users.

Remember, refining and optimizing your product is an ongoing process. Just as with validating your product idea through a no-code MVP, data-driven iterative improvements allow you to respond quickly to your customers' evolving needs and constantly deliver the best possible product.

In conclusion, tracking and analyzing key metrics is critical to the growth and success of your startup. By defining, tracking, and interpreting these metrics, you can continuously improve your no-code MVP and make the right data-driven decisions for a sustainable and thriving business.

7.1 Analyzing User Data: Understand Your Audience and How They Use Your Product

The foundation of data-driven improvements in your No-Code MVP is the ability to analyze your users' behavior and identify areas of improvement, optimization, and growth. To do this, you need to collect and measure data that reflects user interactions with your product. This will enable you to make informed decisions that lead to better user experiences and ultimately, more successful MVPs.

7.1.1 Setting Up Analytics for Your No-Code MVP

To start making data-driven decisions for your MVP, you need to set up some form of analytics to track user interactions. No-code tools usually come with built-in analytics or easy-to-integrate third-party analytics tools, such as Google Analytics, Heap, or Mixpanel.

Here's a simple breakdown of how to set up analytics for some commonly used no-code tools:

- **Webflow** - Webflow provides built-in Google Analytics Integration. All you need to do is enter your tracking ID in the project settings, and Webflow will handle the rest. You can also set up Google Tag Manager for more advanced tracking.
- **Bubble** - Bubble has a built-in analytics feature that provides essential data, such as user count and page views. You can also integrate third-party analytics tools like Google Analytics, Heap, or Mixpanel by adding their tracking code to your app's header or using plugins.

- **Appgyver** - Appgyver allows you to use the JavaScript tracking codes provided by analytics platforms, such as Google Analytics, Heap, or Mixpanel, and directly integrate them into your app's logic. You can also use the REST API feature to fetch data from the analytics tools.
- **Adalo** - Adalo offers a simple interface to add third-party analytics tools like Google Analytics, Mixpanel, or Amplitude to your app. You can add these integrations through the 'External services' section in the app settings.

Remember that when setting up analytics for your No-Code MVP, this can get quite complex, and it is always recommended to seek the guidance of an expert, as you want the data collected to be as accurate and useful as possible.

7.1.2 Identifying Key Performance Indicators (KPIs)

Once you have set-up your analytics platform, the next step is to identify the Key Performance Indicators (KPIs) that matter for your MVP. KPIs are specific, measurable, and actionable metrics that will help you track the performance of your product against your goals. Some commonly used KPIs for No-Code MVPs are:

- User acquisition (e.g., signups, downloads)
- User engagement (e.g., daily active users, session length)
- Retention (e.g., churn rate, daily-to-monthly active users ratio)
- Conversion (e.g., purchases, subscriptions, referrals)
- Revenue (e.g., average revenue per user, monthly recurring revenue)

Each MVP is different, so it's important to identify the KPIs that are most relevant to your unique product and goals. Once you've determined which KPIs to focus on, set up specific tracking events in your analytics platform, so you can measure them accurately and consistently.

7.1.3 Analyzing User Behavior and Identifying Opportunities

With your analytics set up and KPIs defined, you can now monitor user data to understand your audience's behavior and interactions with your No-Code MVP. Keep a close eye on metrics such as:

- Which features are the most popular among users?
- How much time do users spend on specific pages or sections?
- What is the user drop-off in your conversion funnel?
- Which acquisition channels are most effective for driving traffic and user growth?

Use the insights you gather from this data to identify bottlenecks and opportunities for improvement. For example, if you notice a high drop-off rate on your payment page, then it may be worth exploring ways to optimize the payment experience (e.g., reducing friction, offering alternative payment methods, providing more information about secure transactions). Always ensure you are testing any iterations you do make, as you want to continue the path of improvement, not create a negative impact on the user experience.

7.1.4 Running Experiments and A/B Testing

Once you identify areas that require improvements, the next step is to test your hypotheses and measure the impact of your changes. A/B testing, also known as split testing, is an effective way to compare two or more variations of a specific element within your No-Code MVP (e.g., headings, calls to action, landing pages, etc.), to determine which variation performs best.

Here's a simple example of how you can set up an A/B test in a No-Code MVP:

1. **Identify the goal** - Decide the specific business objective you want to achieve with your test. For example, it could be an increase in sign-up conversions, reduced churn rate, or higher engagement.
2. **Design your variations** - Create two or more different versions of the element you want to test (e.g., a landing page with two different headlines or a pricing page with two different offers).
3. **Divide your audience** - Randomly split your user base into equal groups and show each group a different variation of the tested element.
4. **Measure the results** - Monitor the performance of each variation against your KPIs and goals over a set period.
5. **Analyze and iterate** - Use the results from your A/B test to determine the winning variation that achieved your desired goal. Implement the winning version, and continue testing and iterating with different variations.

It's important to note that while A/B testing can be a powerful tool, it can also be resource-intensive, especially for limited-time and resource No-Code MVP projects. Be mindful of the scope and scale of your experiments and prioritize the areas where you expect the most significant impact.

7.1.5 Scaling and Automating Data-Driven Improvements

As you continue to refine and optimize your No-Code MVP, consider exploring advanced data analysis and machine learning tools that can help you gain deeper insights and automate improvements. For example, tools like Google Analytics, Mixpanel, and Amplitude offer advanced features, such as cohort analysis, funnel optimization, and predictive analytics, which can help you uncover hidden patterns and make more informed decisions.

In conclusion, adopting a data-driven approach to making improvements to your No-Code MVP is crucial for its success. By setting up analytics, identifying KPIs, analyzing user behavior, running experiments, and scaling your efforts, you can effectively refine your product, drive user engagement and growth, and ultimately, validate your startup idea. Always remember to iterate based on the data collected, continuously test, and learn from both your successes and failures.

Analyzing User Behavior, Feedback, and Metrics to Drive Growth

One of the key aspects of building a successful No-Code MVP is the ability to make data-driven improvements, refining and optimizing your product to provide the best possible experience for your users. This means going beyond your initial assumptions and carefully analyzing the behaviors, feedback, and metrics from users to continuously improve your product. In this section, we'll discuss the importance of user tracking, data analysis, and optimizing your user experience, as well as exploring various methods and tools that can aid you in gathering the data you need to make informed decisions and iterate on your MVP.

A. User Behavior Tracking

Understanding your users' behavior is crucial to the success of your product. You'll need to learn how users navigate through your product, what features they use the most, and what problems they might be facing. Tracking user behavior will not only provide you with valuable insights but also help you identify specific areas where you can improve the overall experience.

1. Heatmaps

Heatmaps are a visual representation of user interactions on your site or app. They illustrate where users are clicking, scrolling, and spending the most time. This information can be incredibly helpful in identifying problematic UI elements, understanding navigation flows, and even uncovering new opportunities for growth.

There are several No-Code tools available to help you generate heatmaps, such as Hotjar or Crazy Egg. Implementing these tools is usually as simple as adding a piece of code to your website or connecting them to your app through their No-Code integrations.

2. Session Recordings

Session recordings capture and replay individual user sessions on your site or app, allowing you to see exactly what a user did during their visit. This level of detail can help you identify points of friction, usability issues, or areas where users may be struggling.

Tools like FullStory or LogRocket provide No-Code solutions to implement session recording with ease. Integrating them into your MVP will give you invaluable insights that you can use to make targeted improvements to your product.

3. User Flows

User flows represent the paths users take through your product to accomplish specific tasks. Analyzing these flows helps you understand how users interact with your product, uncovering areas where you can improve navigation, streamline processes, or enhance the overall usability.

Tools like Google Analytics, Mixpanel, or Amplitude can help you better understand user flows without requiring any code. By setting up your product with these tools, you can start to gather data on user flows and use it to make iterative improvements.

B. Gathering User Feedback

While tracking user behavior can provide a wealth of insights, it's also important to directly communicate with your users to gather feedback on their experiences. This feedback can help validate or challenge your initial assumptions and provide a clearer path for making improvements.

1. Surveys and Questionnaires

Surveys and questionnaires are an excellent way to gather user feedback at scale. By asking structured, targeted questions, you can gain valuable insights into user satisfaction, feature usage, pain points, and more.

No-Code tools like Typeform, Google Forms, or SurveyMonkey can be easily embedded into your MVP or sent out as standalone forms to collect feedback from your users.

2. Interviews and User Testing Sessions

Conducting one-on-one interviews with users or organizing user testing sessions can give you a more in-depth understanding of user experiences with your product. The conversations and observations during these sessions can help guide your product's ongoing development and reveal opportunities for improvement.

Services like UserTesting or Lookback provide No-Code solutions to recruit participants, set up test environments, and record user testing sessions, making insights from these methods easily accessible.

C. Metrics and KPIs

Identifying and tracking the key performance indicators (KPIs) for your MVP is essential for making clear, data-driven decisions. These metrics can help you understand the overall health of your product, set measurable goals, and evaluate progress over time.

1. Acquisition Metrics

These metrics focus on your ability to attract, engage, and sign up new users. Some key acquisition metrics include:

- Number of new users
- Conversion rate
- Bounce rate

- User acquisition cost

2. Activation Metrics

Activation metrics help you understand how efficiently users are adopting your MVP and benefiting from its core value proposition. Some common activation metrics are:

- Time to first key action
- Onboarding completion rate
- Number of key actions taken

3. Retention Metrics

Retention metrics measure the rate at which users continue using your product after their first experience. These metrics provide insights into the long-term value your MVP provides and can help identify areas for improvement. Some example retention metrics are:

- Churn rate
- Daily/weekly/monthly active users
- Retention rate over time

4. Revenue Metrics

If your MVP is generating revenue or you plan to monetize it in the future, revenue metrics help you track the monetary impact of your product. Important revenue metrics include:

- Average revenue per user
- Lifetime value of a user (LTV)
- Monthly recurring revenue (MRR)

Conclusion

Making data-driven improvements is a crucial step in refining and optimizing your No-Code MVP. By tracking user behavior, gathering user feedback, and monitoring key metrics, you can make informed decisions and iterate on your product, ultimately resulting in a more successful and valuable offering for your users. By leveraging the various No-Code tools and methods discussed above, you'll be well-equipped to harness the power of data and drive growth for your startup.

8. Crafting Your Go-to-Market Strategy: Marketing, Pricing, and Launching

8.1 Crafting Your Go-to-Market Strategy: Marketing, Pricing, and Launching

A go-to-market (GTM) strategy is an essential component to successfully launching your no-code MVP. It is a comprehensive plan that outlines the steps needed to effectively promote, price, and launch your product or service in the market. In this section, we will discuss the key aspects to consider when crafting your go-to-market strategy: marketing, pricing, and launching your MVP.

8.1.1 Marketing Your No-Code MVP

Marketing your no-code MVP is crucial to its success, as it creates awareness, generates user interest, and drives adoption. Here are the key considerations for marketing your MVP without breaking the bank:

1. Define your target audience: Start by identifying your ideal customers; who are they, and what are their needs, preferences, and pain points? You can use personas, market segmentation, or other customer profiling techniques to narrow down your focus.

2. Develop your value proposition: Clearly articulate the unique benefits your MVP brings to your target audience. This statement should highlight the essential features and differentiators of your product and explain why it solves their problem better than any alternative.

3. Craft your messaging: Develop the core messages that you will use in your marketing campaigns. Keep the language simple and concise, focusing on the benefits and outcomes of using your product, while addressing the concerns and interests of your target audience.

4. Build a basic online presence: A minimal and clean website or a landing page can make a significant first impression on potential users. Include essential information about your product, your value proposition, and a clear call to action for visitors to sign up or learn more.

5. Leverage content marketing: Creating useful and valuable content for your target audience is a powerful way to generate traction. Write blog posts, whitepapers, or create videos and webinars to educate your audience on the problem you solve and the benefits of your solution.

6. Engage in social media marketing: Use appropriate social media channels to share your content and engage in a conversation with your target audience. Social media can be an effective and cost-efficient way to promote your MVP and build a community of early adopters.

7. Network and utilize partnerships: Attend relevant events and conferences, join online communities, and collaborate with influencers or complementary businesses in your industry to expand your reach.

8.1.2 Pricing Your No-Code MVP

Determining the right price for your MVP can be challenging, but the following factors can serve as a guide to help you make decisions:

1. Understand your customers' willingness to pay: Conduct surveys, interviews, or focus groups with your target audience to understand their perceived value of your product and their price expectations.

2. Analyze competitor pricing: Research your competitors' pricing strategies and understand where your product stands in the market landscape comparison. This knowledge can help you position your MVP at a competitive price point.

3. Consider different pricing models: There are various pricing models to choose from, such as free, one-time purchase, subscription, tiered (based on features, users or usage), or freemium (free with premium features for a price). Select the model that best aligns with your customers' preferences and your business goals.

4. Start with an initial price and be flexible: While pricing your MVP, it's essential to be open to adjustments based on your customers' feedback and market response. Be prepared to iterate on your pricing strategy as necessary.

8.1.3 Launching Your No-Code MVP

A well-planned launch strategy can make all the difference for your no-code MVP's success. Keep these guidelines in mind for a smooth launch:

1. Set measurable goals: Establish quantifiable and time-bound objectives for your launch. For example, "Acquire 100 beta users within two weeks after launch" or "Generate 10% conversion rate from free trial to paid customers within one month after launch."

2. Develop a pre-launch plan: Create buzz around your MVP before the big day by nurturing your network, engaging with relevant communities, and starting teaser campaigns or pre-launch offers.

3. Implement a soft launch: Before going public, conduct a soft-launch to a smaller audience, or invite-only beta testing. This will help you gather valuable feedback, iron out any last-minute issues, and ensure that your product runs smoothly when it hits the market.

4. Coordinate a multi-channel marketing campaign: Plan and execute a marketing campaign that includes various tactics such as email, PR, content marketing, influencer outreach, or even paid advertising to amplify your launch and reach a broader audience.

5. Provide excellent customer support: Improve your user experience and retention by offering personal and prompt customer support, addressing feedback, and iteratively enhancing your product based on user insights.

Overall, crafting a solid go-to-market strategy plays a vital role in ensuring that your no-code MVP gains traction and delivers value to your target audience. By following these recommendations on marketing, pricing, and launching your product, you will be well on your way to validating your startup idea and moving closer to success.

Crafting Your Go-to-Market Strategy: Marketing, Pricing, and Launching

Developing a No-Code MVP is an effective way to quickly build and validate startup ideas. However, even the most viable product will not gain traction without the right marketing strategy, pricing model, and launch plan. In this section, we will explore the key components to crafting an effective go-to-market strategy for your No-Code MVP.

Marketing: Building Awareness and Driving Engagement

The primary goal of marketing is to generate interest in your product, and ultimately, convert that interest into sales or user adoption. For your No-Code MVP, it's crucial to develop a marketing plan that targets your core audience and clearly communicates the value proposition of your product.

1. **Define your target audience**: Begin by identifying the specific customer segments that will benefit the most from your product. Create detailed personas that include demographic, psychographic and behavioral information about your ideal customers.
2. **Develop key messaging**: Your messaging should focus on the problem-solving aspects of your product and clearly articulate its unique value proposition. Use simple language to ensure your audience understands your product's purpose and benefits.
3. **Choose the right channels**: Identify the platforms where your target audience is most active and engaged, such as social media, industry forums, or

email lists. Focus your marketing efforts on these channels to reach potential customers more effectively.

4. **Create valuable content**: Develop educational materials, such as blog posts, videos, and webinars, focused on your target audience's pain points and how your product can address them. This approach not only helps to establish your brand as an authority in your industry but also drives organic traffic to your website.
5. **Leverage partnerships**: Seek out partnerships with influencers, industry experts, and complementary businesses in your niche to increase your product's visibility and credibility.
6. **Measure success**: Track engagement, conversions, and overall effectiveness of your marketing efforts using analytics tools. Modify your marketing plan as needed to maximize your return on investment.

Pricing: Finding the Sweet Spot

Selecting the appropriate pricing model for your No-Code MVP is critical, as it can significantly impact the adoption of your product. Here are some steps to help you determine the best pricing strategy:

1. **Conduct market research**: Investigate the pricing models of competitors, as well as any industry standards. This information will provide you with a baseline and a better understanding of your customers' expectations.
2. **Understand your costs**: Calculate the total cost of developing and maintaining your product, including development, infrastructure, and ongoing support. This will help you establish the minimum price

necessary to cover these expenses and remain profitable.

3. **Optimize for value**: Your product's price should be reflective of the value it delivers to customers. Consider conducting surveys or user testing to understand the perceived value of your product and compare that to your competitors' offerings.
4. **Test different pricing models**: Experiment with various pricing models, such as freemium, subscription, or one-time payment, to determine which best suits your target audience's preferences and your business goals.
5. **Offer promotions**: Attract early adopters and generate buzz around your product by offering limited-time promotions, such as discounts or exclusive access to premium features for early subscribers.

Launching: Timing and Execution

The success of your No-Code MVP can be heavily influenced by the timing and execution of your product launch. Here are some tips for a successful launch:

1. **Prepare for launch**: Before announcing your product, ensure that your MVP is stable, polished, and ready for user feedback. Also, have a plan in place for addressing any potential technical issues that may arise post-launch.
2. **Choose the right timing**: Select a launch date that maximizes the attention of your target audience and avoids conflicts with major industry events or holidays.
3. **Build anticipation**: Create a pre-launch campaign to generate excitement around your product. Share teasers on social media, release valuable content that

highlights your product's features, and encourage your audience to sign up for early access or join a waiting list.

4. **Leverage your network**: Reach out to your personal and professional network for support during the launch. Encourage them to share your product with their own networks, write reviews, or provide testimonials.

5. **Monitor and adjust**: After launching, track user feedback, engagement, and any technical issues that may arise. Use this information to iterate on your No-Code MVP quickly and make improvements.

In conclusion, the success of your No-Code MVP depends not only on the viability of your product idea but also on your go-to-market strategy. A solid marketing plan, appropriate pricing model, and well-executed launch will significantly increase your chances of success and help you turn your No-Code MVP into a thriving business.

8. Crafting Your Go-to-Market Strategy: Marketing, Pricing, and Launching

In this chapter, we will delve into the realm of crafting a successful go-to-market strategy for your no-code MVP. In doing so, we will explore the following key aspects: marketing your product, pricing it accurately and effectively, and finally, launching your MVP to the masses.

8.1 Marketing Strategy

A well-executed marketing strategy is critical for creating awareness around your product and attracting potential customers. Consider the following tactics when devising your marketing plan for your no-code MVP:

8.1.1 Establishing a Brand Identity

Before you embark on your marketing journey, it is crucial to establish a strong brand identity. Your brand identity should answer the following questions:

- Who are you?
- What is your mission?
- What sets your product apart from the competition?

Once you have addressed these questions, you can create a fitting logo, tone, and color scheme that will resonate with your target audience.

8.1.2 Identifying Target Audiences

To optimize your marketing efforts, identify and segment your target audiences based on their common traits such as demographics, interests, and pain points. This will enable you to send tailored marketing messages that resonate deeply with different groups and foster a deeper connection with your brand.

8.1.3 Content Marketing

Content marketing is a highly effective way to establish brand authority, educate your target audience, and engage potential customers. Utilize various formats such as blog posts, eBooks, infographics, podcasts, and video content, and distribute them across different channels like social media, email marketing, and your website.

8.1.4 Social Media Marketing

Harness the power of social media platforms to create brand awareness, gather feedback, and engage with your audience. Focus on platforms where your target audience is most active and strive to maintain a consistent brand presence with a content calendar.

8.1.5 Community Building

Building a community around your brand can significantly amplify your marketing efforts. Engage with users on social media, participate in relevant forums, and create a space for your audience to connect—for example, through Facebook or Slack groups.

8.2 Pricing Strategy

Setting the right pricing strategy for your no-code MVP can significantly impact its success. Consider the following factors when devising your pricing plan:

8.2.1 Know Your Costs

Before setting a price for your MVP, you must be fully aware of the costs associated with creating and maintaining the product. Factors to consider include production costs, infrastructure costs, and any other operational expenses.

8.2.2 Conduct Market Research

Research the competitive landscape to get a better understanding of industry pricing standards. Look for any pricing gaps in the market that your MVP can fill while still remaining profitable.

8.2.3 Test Different Pricing Models

Experiment with different pricing models to determine the one that works best for your product. Some common pricing strategies include:

- Free-mium: Offer a basic version of your product for free with the option for users to upgrade to a premium, feature-rich version for a fee.
- Subscription-based: Charge users a recurring fee for access to your product, typically on a monthly or annual basis.
- Pay-as-you-go: Bill users based on usage, where higher usage results in increased fees.

8.3 Launch Strategy

The launch of your no-code MVP is a crucial milestone that requires careful planning and execution. To ensure a successful launch, consider the following tips:

8.3.1 Build Anticipation

Generate excitement for your product launch by releasing a series of teasers, product demonstrations, and pre-launch offers. Build an email list of interested prospects and keep them informed about the product's development, upcoming features, and official launch date.

8.3.2 Organize a Launch Event

Organizing a launch event can provide you with valuable exposure and validation for your no-code MVP. You can host a virtual event on social media, a webinar, or collaborate with industry influencers to promote your MVP extensively.

8.3.3 Iterate and Improve

No product is perfect at launch. Encourage user feedback and continuously update and refine your product based on the insights gathered. User reviews and success stories can serve as powerful marketing content for future campaigns.

In conclusion, a well-crafted go-to-market strategy that incorporates marketing, pricing, and launching techniques can maximize your no-code MVP's success. By tailoring your message to your target audience, selecting a fitting pricing strategy, and launching your product with a splash, you pave the way for the successful growth of your no-code startup.

8. Crafting Your Go-to-Market Strategy: Marketing, Pricing, and Launching

One of the most significant determinants of your startup's success is your go-to-market (GTM) strategy. A GTM strategy outlines how your product will reach and engage your target customers, which directly influences your bottom line. This requires understanding your target audience, determining effective marketing channels, pricing strategies, and an impactful launch plan to validate and scale your No-Code MVP.

8.1 Determine Your Target Audience

Your target audience is the group of customers that your MVP aims to serve. These are the people who will benefit the most from your product, and would be willing to pay for it. It is essential to understand your audience—a task that can be broken down into two parts:

1. **Demographics**: The demographic profile of your target audience includes characteristics such as age,

gender, occupation, income levels, and location. You can use these signals to develop your marketing strategy and make your messaging more relevant to specific customer segments.

2. **Psychographics**: This refers to the attitudes, beliefs, preferences, and motivations of your target audience. Understanding psychographics helps you better connect with your audience, tailor your marketing message, and design features that resonate with potential customers.

Ask yourself these key questions to define your target audience:

- Who are the people facing the problem that our MVP solves?
- What are their needs, preferences, and behaviors?
- How would they benefit from our product or service?

8.2 Select Your Marketing Channels

Once you have a clear understanding of your target audience, it is time to identify the best marketing channels to reach them. These can include:

- **Content Marketing**: Publishing blog posts, articles, and other content that highlights your product and showcases your expertise in the field. This helps build trust, engage your audience, and attracts organic search traffic over time.
- **Email Marketing**: Compose regular newsletters or updates to connect with potential and existing customers. Offer valuable insights, updates about product features, or exclusive promotions to keep your audience engaged with your brand.

- **Social Media Marketing**: Make use of various social media platforms like Facebook, LinkedIn, and Twitter to showcase your brand personality, drive engagement, and create buzz about your MVP.
- **Influencer/PR Outreach**: Partner with influencers, bloggers, and media outlets for product promotion, reviews, and endorsements. This is a cost-effective way to drive awareness and credibility for your brand.
- **Paid Advertising**: Use targeted ads on search engines (like Google Ads) or social media platforms (like Facebook, Twitter, or LinkedIn) to reach your target customers more quickly.

8.3 Establish Your Pricing Strategy

Pricing is a crucial factor in attracting and retaining customers. A well-defined pricing strategy ensures that your target audience perceives the value of your offering and is willing to pay for it. You can consider pricing models like:

- **Freemium**: Provide access to a basic version of your product for free while offering paid plans with additional features. This can help acquire and engage a large user base, and drive conversions to paid plans over time.
- **Subscription**: Charge a recurring fee for access to your product or service. This allows users to pay for continued usage and helps build a predictable revenue stream for your business.
- **Pay-per-use**: Charge users based on their actual usage of the product. This can make it more attractive to potential customers who don't want long-term commitments or upfront fees.

When selecting the right pricing model for your MVP, consider the competitive landscape, your target audience's willingness to pay, and your operational costs.

8.4 Launch Your No-Code MVP

Now that you have your target audience, marketing, and pricing strategies in place, it's time to launch your MVP. The goal here is to validate your hypotheses, acquire early customers, and gather initial user feedback. To ensure a successful launch, keep the following points in mind:

1. **Plan Ahead**: Assemble a launch timeline that includes pre-launch marketing activities, traction goals, and what you want to learn from the initial user feedback.
2. **Pre-launch Activities**: Share sneak peeks, teasers, or beta invites to generate hype about your product. Connect with influencers, bloggers, or media contacts to secure coverage during the launch.
3. **Optimize Your Website**: Make sure your website has clear messaging, call-to-actions, and a straightforward onboarding process to help new users understand your value proposition quickly.
4. **Track Metrics**: Monitor the key performance indicators (KPIs) for your MVP post-launch, including user acquisition rates, conversion rates, retention, and user feedback. These insights will help improve your product, marketing strategy, and inform your next steps.

Remember that the launch of your MVP is just the starting point. Continuous improvement based on user feedback and data-driven optimization will keep your product competitive and maximize its potential for long-term success.

8.1 Crafting Your Go-to-Market Strategy: Marketing, Pricing, and Launching

Once your No-Code MVP (Minimum Viable Product) is ready, it's time to introduce it to the market. Crafting an effective go-to-market (GTM) strategy includes marketing, pricing, and launching your product. In this section, we'll cover various aspects of each of these critical elements, which will help you not only reach more potential customers but also maximize your chances of a successful launch.

8.1.1 Developing the Marketing Strategy

Developing a comprehensive marketing strategy is essential when launching your MVP. To start, you'll want to consider the following areas:

1. **Target Market & Personas**: The first step is to identify your target market and create buyer personas. Knowing your target audience will help you tailor your messaging and select the most relevant marketing channels. Create detailed buyer personas, which include demographics, behavior patterns, and goals.
2. **Competitive Analysis**: Analyze your competition and identify their strengths and weaknesses. This information will help you understand your product's unique selling propositions (USPs). It will also enable you to communicate these USPs to your target audience effectively.
3. **Marketing Channels**: Identifying appropriate marketing channels is crucial. Consider using organic (SEO, content marketing, social media) and paid channels (Google Ads, Facebook Ads) or any other channels relevant to your target audience.

4. **Messaging & Positioning**: Create unique messaging that sets your product apart from your competition. Your messaging should be clear, concise, and directly address the needs of your target audience. Also, focus on emphasizing your product's USPs.
5. **Budget & Timeline**: Determine the budget required for your marketing initiatives and develop a timeline that outlines the sequence of tasks and milestones.

8.1.2 Setting the Right Pricing Strategy

Setting the right price for your product is critical to its success in the market. There are six core strategies that you can use to price your product:

1. **Cost-Plus Pricing**: Calculate the total costs of creating your product and add a percentage markup to account for profit.
2. **Competitive Pricing**: Set your price based on your competitors' pricing.
3. **Value-Based Pricing**: Determine the price based on the value your product adds to your customers.
4. **Freemium Pricing**: Offer a basic version of the product for free, with additional features available for a fee.
5. **Tiered or Variable Pricing**: Offer different pricing levels with varying features and capabilities.
6. **Penetration Pricing**: Introduce the product at a low price to attract customers initially, then increase the price over time.

Consider using a combination of these strategies to set an attractive but profitable price for your MVP.

8.1.3 Pre-Launch Activities

Before you launch your MVP, there are several pre-launch activities you should engage in:

1. **Building a Pre-Launch List**: Create a landing page to collect email addresses and build a list of potential customers who are interested in your product.
2. **Public Relations (PR)**: Reach out to relevant media outlets, influencers, and bloggers to secure coverage or mentions of your product.
3. **Content Marketing**: Create valuable content (blog posts, ebooks, webinars, etc.) targeting your target audience and addressing their needs or challenges.
4. **Social Media**: Engage your target audience on relevant social media platforms through consistent posting, engaging, and sharing content.
5. **Email Marketing**: Send personalized emails to your pre-launch list to provide updates, share content, and create excitement about your upcoming product launch.

8.1.4 Launching Your MVP

Once you've completed your pre-launch activities, it's time to launch your MVP:

1. **Soft Launch**: A soft launch allows you to test your product with a small group of customers before the official launch. It helps you identify any issues, gather feedback, and make improvements to your MVP based on real-life scenarios.
2. **Public Launch**: After addressing the feedback received during the soft launch, you can proceed with the public launch. Make sure you've updated your marketing materials, website, and landing page with the latest information.

3. **Outreach & Promotion**: Execute your marketing strategy by engaging in outreach and promoting your product across your chosen marketing channels.
4. **Track & Measure**: Monitor the performance of your MVP using key performance indicators (KPIs) like downloads, sign-ups, engagement, and revenue.
5. **Iterate & Optimize**: Analyze the results, gather customer feedback, and continuously adjust your marketing strategy, product features, and pricing to optimize the performance of your MVP.

In conclusion, crafting a comprehensive GTM strategy that encompasses marketing, pricing, and effective launch tactics will not only ensure a successful launch but also maximize the potential of your No-Code MVP. Taking the time to research your target market, design the proper promotional campaign, and implement an effective strategy will put your product on the path to success.

9. Scaling Your Startup with No-Code: Growth Strategies and Advanced Techniques

9.2 Advanced Techniques in No-Code for Scaling Your Startup

Once you've successfully built and validated your idea using a no-code Minimum Viable Product (MVP), the next step is to scale your startup. Scaling means growing your user base, increasing your revenue, and optimizing your operations. With no-code tools at your disposal, you can successfully execute growth strategies and advanced techniques without writing a single line of code.

9.2.1 Automate Your Operations

Automation can help in reducing manual efforts and streamlining your operations. Many no-code tools offer integrations and automation options that help you connect different aspects of your business, making them run more efficiently.

Zapier

Zapier is a no-code automation platform. It allows businesses to integrate multiple apps and automate their workflows. With a library of over 2,000 apps, including popular services like Slack, Trello, and Gmail, Zapier makes it easy to create custom automations without needing any programming knowledge.

Instead of spending time on repetitive tasks, such as manually entering information into spreadsheets or sending out emails, you can set up a "Zap" to do the job for you automatically.

Integromat

Integromat is another no-code automation platform that helps you automate your workflows. It's similar to Zapier, but it offers a more visual way to create complex integrations with a wide range of apps and services. Integromat also provides more advanced features, such as error handling and custom logic functions that can be added to your workflow.

9.2.2 Increase Revenue with No-Code Analytics and Conversion Rate Optimization

Unlocking the power of data is essential for scaling your startup. With no-code analytics and conversion rate optimization tools, you can make data-driven decisions without the need for technical expertise.

Google Analytics

Google Analytics is a popular no-code analytics tool that helps you better understand your website traffic and audience behavior. It allows you to analyze data and make improvements to your website, which in turn can lead to higher conversion rates and increased revenue.

Hotjar

Hotjar is a no-code tool that helps you understand user behavior on your website. Using heatmaps, visitor recordings, and conversion funnels, Hotjar provides insights that can help you optimize your site and increase revenue.

Optimizely

Optimizely is a no-code platform for conducting A/B testing and personalizing your website to improve user experience and conversion rates. It offers an easy-to-use interface for creating experiments, analyzing results, and implementing data-driven changes to your website.

9.2.3 Streamline and Scale Customer Onboarding and Support

Scaling also means having the infrastructure and processes in place to handle a growing number of customers. No-code tools can help you automate, streamline, and scale customer onboarding and support.

Intercom

Intercom is a no-code platform for managing customer communications. It offers a suite of tools for customer support, messaging, and engagement, allowing you to proactively and efficiently manage your growing user base.

Typeform

Typeform is a no-code tool for creating engaging, conversational forms and surveys. It lets you build beautiful, mobile-optimized forms that can be used for customer feedback, lead generation, and more.

HelpScout

HelpScout is a no-code help desk and customer support platform. It provides a shared inbox for your team to manage and track incoming customer queries, offering quick and personalized support.

9.2.4 Tools and Strategies for Scaling User Acquisition

Growing your user base is paramount to scaling your startup. With no-code user acquisition tools and strategies, you can attract more users to your product while keeping acquisition costs low.

Mailchimp

Mailchimp is a no-code email marketing platform. It allows you to create personalized and targeted email campaigns, which can help drive more users to your startup.

Buffer/Pablo

Buffer is a no-code social media management platform that helps you schedule, publish, and analyze your social media content. Pablo by Buffer is a no-code graphic design tool to create engaging social media images quickly.

Unbounce

Unbounce is a no-code landing page builder that allows you to create high-converting landing pages for your marketing campaigns, driving more signups and users.

9.2.5 Keep Experimenting and Iterating

Finally, scaling your startup is an ongoing process for which iteration is key. Continuously experimenting with new growth strategies while using no-code tools to test, analyze, and optimize will help you stay ahead of the competition and keep your startup growing.

Leveraging advanced no-code techniques and tools enables you to scale your startup effectively through automation, analytics, conversion rate optimization, and user acquisition strategies. Keep iterating and experimenting to find the best combination of tools and tactics that work for your specific needs and goals, ensuring your startup's growth and success.

9.1 Utilizing Advanced No-Code Tools and Integrations for Growth

Once you've achieved a certain level of traction and product-market fit with your no-code MVP, it's time to shift your focus towards scaling your startup. No-code platforms and tools enable business owners to implement growth strategies and advanced techniques without the need to rely on a technical team, which makes scaling more efficient and cost-effective. In this section, we'll dive into the specifics of how you can leverage powerful non-code tools to scale your startup.

9.1.1 Automate Your Workflows

Automation is the key to scaling a business efficiently. As your startup grows, it gets increasingly challenging to manage and track everything manually. No-code tools such as Zapier, Integromat, and N8n enable you to automate your workflows and eliminate routine tasks, saving you and your team hours of valuable time to focus on more important tasks.

To begin automating your startup, identify your most time-consuming procedures and tasks, such as onboarding new clients, sending follow-up emails, managing social media posts, and tracking leads. Use automation tools to create custom workflows that streamline these tasks with predefined criteria.

9.1.2 Analytics and User Engagement

Advanced analytics and user engagement tools are essential for understanding user behavior, identifying areas of improvement, and monitoring your startup's growth. Tools like Google Analytics, Mixpanel, and Hotjar provide essential insights about your users, allowing you to make data-driven decisions to tweak and refine your product or service.

In addition, use no-code analytics tools to set up custom conversion goals, monitor user acquisition channels, and optimize your marketing and sales funnels. This way, you can accurately track your growth and make informed decisions about how to allocate your time and resources to maximize ROI.

9.1.3 Customize and Optimize Your Marketing Strategies

With no-code tools, you can easily create and test various marketing strategies and campaigns, measuring their impact on your growth, and optimizing them for better conversions. Utilize platforms like MailChimp, ConvertKit, and HubSpot to create email automation sequences, perform A/B testing, and personalize your interactions with users.

In addition, consider leveraging social media management tools like Buffer, Hootsuite, and SocialBee to schedule and maintain a consistent online presence across platforms. These tools can also help you manage and analyze your social media data, enabling you to adapt your messaging and content to your audience's preferences.

9.1.4 Harness the Power of Community Building

An engaged and loyal community can contribute immensely to a startup's growth. Building a passionate community around your product or service helps with user retention, expands your reach, and provides valuable insights into user needs, preferences, and pain points.

Leverage tools like Circle, Tribe, or Discord to create a no-code community platform where your customers can interact with each other and your team. Engage in meaningful discussions, solicit valuable feedback, and provide exclusive member benefits to foster community loyalty.

9.1.5 Incorporate AI and Machine Learning

Advanced technologies like artificial intelligence and machine learning can be game-changers for your startup's growth. No-code tools like AlwaysAI, Open.AI, or DataRobot can add powerful AI features to your product or service without the need for dedicated experts on your team.

For example, you can use AI chatbots to enhance customer support, create personalized experiences with machine learning, or automate content creation using natural language processing tools. Harness the potential of these advanced technologies with no-code platforms to stay ahead of the competition.

9.1.6 Continually Iterate and Improve Your Product

As your startup scales, continually iterate and enhance your product based on user feedback and data insights. Utilize advanced no-code tools like SurveySparrow, Typeform, or Bravo Studio to collect user feedback, conduct surveys, and prototype new features. With no-code solutions, you can rapidly release new iterations, reduce development time, and stay agile in responding to your customers' needs and preferences.

9.1.7 Summary

Scaling your startup with no-code means leveraging advanced tools, technologies, and integrations to optimize efficiency and drive growth. Continuously experiment with new strategies, refine processes, and embrace a data-driven mentality. Utilize the power of no-code platforms to stay agile, adaptive, and responsive to both customer and market demands, empowering your startup's overall success.

By harnessing the capabilities of no-code tools for automation, analytics, marketing, community building, AI integration, and rapid product iteration, you can effectively scale your startup, create a sustainable competitive advantage, and turn your MVP into a thriving business.

Automating Processes for Scalability

As your startup begins to grow, manual processes that seemed manageable in the beginning can quickly become time-consuming and hinder your ability to scale efficiently. Identifying these processes and finding ways to automate them without code can save you time and resources, helping you grow even faster.

In this section, we will explore some popular no-code automation tools and how they can help improve processes within your startup.

Zapier: Workflow Automation

Zapier is one of the most popular no-code automation tools available. It connects thousands of apps and automates workflows between them, saving you the time and hassle of manual data entry and updates.

By creating what Zapier calls "Zaps," you can automate various tasks based on triggers and actions between supported apps. For example, you can create a Zap that triggers when someone fills out a form on your website and then automatically adds their information to your CRM or email marketing software.

Here are a few potential use cases for automating processes with Zapier:

- Automatically create a new Trello card, Asana task, or Monday.com board item when a new feature request or bug report is submitted
- Move completed tasks into relevant project management software, folders, or stages upon completion
- Sync contacts and customer data from your CRM to your email marketing software or conversely, from your email marketing software to your CRM
- Receive notifications in Slack when critical events happen, such as new user sign-ups, product sales, or important website form submissions
- Automate social media scheduling by connecting tools like Buffer or Hootsuite to your content calendar

Integromat: Visual Automation Builder

Integromat is another no-code automation tool that offers a visual builder to create automation workflows. Like Zapier, Integromat connects various apps and services to automate tasks, but with added flexibility in terms of data manipulation and multi-step workflows.

With Integromat's drag-and-drop interface, you can visually map how data is transferred and transformed between different apps. While this may be more advanced than

Zapier, it provides greater control over your workflows and can handle more sophisticated automation use cases.

Integromat can help you automate processes like:

- Complex data transformations and calculations between apps (e.g., calculating a customer's lifetime value before syncing it with your CRM)
- Creating an automated onboarding sequence for new users, including tasks like sending a welcome email, adding them to a relevant email sequence, and assigning a team member to follow up with them personally
- Tracking and analyzing website events, such as user visits, button clicks, or purchases, to optimize the user experience and increase conversions

Tools for Automating Customer Support

Customer support is often time-consuming and labor-intensive, and as your startup grows, providing responsive and efficient support can prove increasingly challenging. However, there are several no-code tools that can help you streamline your support services:

- **Intercom**: Intercom is a customer communication platform that offers a range of features designed to facilitate better customer engagement and support. One such feature is Operator, an AI-powered chatbot that can automatically answer common customer questions, schedule meetings, or route conversations to the appropriate team members.
- **ManyChat**: ManyChat lets you create Facebook Messenger chatbots to automate customer support, sales, and marketing. By setting up automated workflows, you can answer frequently asked

questions, collect leads, or even complete purchase procedures directly within Messenger.

- **HelpDocs**: HelpDocs is a knowledge base platform that makes it quick and straightforward to create and organize help articles for your users. A well-organized knowledge base empowers your customers to find answers to their questions independently, reducing the volume of support tickets and saving your team time.

Conclusion

As your startup scales, the need for automation grows. Embracing the no-code movement and incorporating no-code automation tools and growth strategies into your business not only allows you to streamline processes for efficiency but also frees up time for you and your team to focus on new ideas and improvements.

No-code automation empowers you to grow and scale your startup without sacrificing quality or incurring additional technical debt. As you continue on this journey, stay curious about new tools, technologies, and techniques that make scaling more accessible, more efficient, and more cost-effective.

9.1 Leveraging No-Code Tools for Growth Strategies

Growing your startup requires not only scaling your user base but also increasing customer satisfaction, retention, and revenue. The good news is that no-code tools can help you execute growth strategies and advanced techniques without hiring a larger development team or spending months learning to code. In this section, we'll outline several strategies to help grow your startup and explore how no-code tools can be leveraged to implement them efficiently.

1. Optimize Your Onboarding Experience

Your onboarding experience is crucial for converting new users into engaged customers. A smooth onboarding process can reduce churn and improve user retention. No-code tools can help you create a streamlined onboarding flow that guides users through your product's features and encourages them to take action.

- **Tutorial and Walkthroughs:** No-code tools like UserGuiding and Usetiful allow you to create interactive tutorials and walkthroughs without any coding. You can show users exactly how to use your product and educate them on its unique features.
- **User Feedback:** Collecting feedback from users during the onboarding process can help you improve your product and address any users' pain points. No-code tools like Hotjar and UserVoice allow you to collect and analyze user feedback, so you can make data-driven decisions to optimize your onboarding experience.

2. Increase User Engagement

Investing in user engagement strategies can help increase your product's usage and empower users to find more value in your offering over time. Leverage no-code tools to create gamification systems, personalized user experiences, or notification campaigns to re-engage users.

- **Gamification:** Incentivizing users to take desired actions or rewarding them for their achievements can help increase user engagement. No-code tools like Gleam or SailPlay can help you create gamification systems, such as point systems, badges, and leaderboards, without any coding.
- **Personalized User Experiences:** Tailoring your product's content based on your users' preferences and behavior can create a more compelling user experience. No-code tools like Segment and Optimizely can help you create personalized user experiences based on factors like user location, device type, or previous interactions.
- **Notification Campaigns:** Sending notifications to users based on their behavior or inactivity can help keep them engaged with your product. Many no-code tools, such as OneSignal and Pusher, allow you to send notifications via email or mobile devices based on specific actions or events.

3. Automate Marketing and Sales

Automating your startup's marketing and sales efforts can save you time and resources while increasing your capacity to reach more customers. No-code tools can help you automate various stages of your sales funnel, from lead generation to nurturing and onboarding.

- **Email Automation:** Sending personalized, automated emails based on user behavior or interaction with your product can help you nurture leads and convert users into customers. No-code tools like Mailchimp and ActiveCampaign can help you set up automated email sequences to keep users engaged.

- **Social Media Automation:** No-code tools like Hootsuite and Buffer can help you efficiently manage and schedule your social media posts, allowing you to maintain a consistent presence on social platforms.
- **Lead Generation:** No-code tools like Typeform and Landbot can help you create engaging forms and chatbots to collect user information and generate leads for your sales team.
- **CRM Integration:** Integrating your no-code tools with popular CRM platforms like Salesforce or HubSpot can help you manage and analyze customer data, identify sales opportunities, and close deals more efficiently.

4. Optimize Your Website and Product for Conversion

Improving your website's conversion rate can have a significant impact on your startup's growth. By testing and optimizing your landing pages, user flows, and calls to action, you can increase the number of visitors converting into customers.

- **A/B Testing:** No-code tools like Optimizely and Google Optimize can help you create and run A/B tests to evaluate different variations of your website or app and identify the best-performing design, copy, or user flow.
- **Heatmaps and Click Tracking:** Tools like Hotjar or Crazy Egg can help you track where users click, scroll, or hover on your website, providing valuable insights into potential areas for improvement.
- **Conversion Rate Optimization (CRO):** No-code platforms like Unbounce or Instapage can help you

design and publish highly optimized landing pages focused on improving your conversion rates.

By leveraging no-code tools in these growth strategies, you can efficiently scale your startup, focusing on improving user experiences and maximizing revenue while reducing time spent on development tasks. Time saved can be used to think strategically and create further opportunities for growth.

Building a Scalable Business Infrastructure

As your startup begins to grow, it becomes increasingly important to have a scalable business infrastructure in place. This means optimizing your workflows, growing your customer base, expanding into new markets, and being able to adapt quickly to changes in the business environment. With no-code tools, you can streamline and automate many aspects of your operations, increasing your efficiency and ensuring your business remains agile.

1. Streamline Your Workflows

A key component of scaling your startup is optimizing and streamlining your workflows. As the number of users, customers, and team members increases, tasks and communication can become more complex and disorganized. The powerful functionality of no-code tools can help you manage this:

- Automate repetitive tasks: Your team might be wasting valuable time on tasks that can be automated. With no-code tools like Zapier, you can automate repetitive tasks such as updating your CRM or sending emails, freeing up time and resources for more important tasks.

- Streamline project management: Keep track of multiple projects and ensure that your team is aligned with their goals by using no-code project management tools, such as Trello, ClickUp, and Notion. By automating processes and efficiently managing your team's time, you will increase productivity and reduce the risk of bottlenecks.
- Integrate your apps: As your business grows, you'll likely use more tools to manage different aspects of your operations. No-code platforms like Integromat allow you to integrate different applications and automate data flows between them. By centralizing your data, you can make better decisions and automate more of your operations.

2. Customer Outreach and Engagement

Your startup's growth depends on continuously attracting new customers and retaining existing ones. Connect with potential customers and strengthen existing relationships by enhancing your digital presence and leveraging data.

- Build robust email campaigns: Automated email campaigns can help you engage with your audience, generate new leads, and increase your revenue. Tools like Mailchimp allow you to create, manage, and optimize your email campaigns without any coding knowledge, making it easier for startups to scale their marketing efforts.
- Empower data-driven decision making: To effectively scale, it's important to understand your target audience and their behavior. Tools like Google Analytics and Mixpanel let you track and analyze user behavior on your website or app, while no-code tools

like Airtable allow you to organize, analyze, and visualize customer data. By understanding your customers better, you can adjust marketing and growth strategies to optimize performance.

3. Exploring New Markets

A successful scaling strategy often includes expanding to new markets. With no-code tools, you can quickly build and test your efforts before committing valuable resources.

- Translate your website: Translate your website and make it more accessible to users in different markets by using no-code translation tools like Weglot or Localize.
- Create localized landing pages: Use a no-code website builder like Webflow to create dedicated landing pages for new markets. Test different messaging, positioning, and visuals to analyze which resonates best with each new audience.

4. Strengthening Your Financial Backbone

As your business grows, it's crucial to effectively manage your financials. No-code tools can help you automate your financial processes and get a better understanding of your startup's overall financial health.

- Automate your invoicing and accounting: Tools like QuickBooks or Xero can help you automate and simplify your bookkeeping, invoicing, and expense tracking.

- Project your finances: Use no-code platforms like Finmark to build financial models and project your future revenue, expenses, and cash flow. This will help you better understand your startup's financial health and make informed decisions about hiring, fundraising, and resource allocation.

5. Responding to Change

No matter how well you plan, the business environment will likely always throw surprises at you. Being agile and adapting quickly to changes can be the key to continued growth.

- Continuously iterate and improve your product: Use no-code tools like Bubble or Adalo to make ongoing updates and improvements to your product without needing to rely on developers.
- Monitor your competition: Stay ahead of your competitors by tracking their marketing strategies and product offerings. Use tools like SimilarWeb and BuiltWith to evaluate their digital presence and technology stack.

By leveraging no-code tools and implementing strategies for growth, you can quickly scale your startup without the need for extensive technical resources or knowledge. As your business grows, it's essential to continuously iterate, adapt, and optimize. Investing in no-code tools not only allows you to respond quickly to change but also frees up resources to focus on the areas that will drive the most growth for your business.

10. Case Studies: Real-World No-Code MVP Success Stories

Case Study 1: Glide Apps – Creating a Local Business Directory

The Problem

Joe, an aspiring entrepreneur, recognized a gap in the market for a local business directory that could help people find and support small businesses in his town during the COVID-19 pandemic. He had noticed that many residents struggled to find local shops and service providers amidst the decline of print directories and the rise of larger e-commerce platforms.

The Idea

Joe decided to create a digital directory that would compile information about local businesses, making it easy for users to find and contact them. He envisioned a mobile app that included features such as categories, location-based services, and customer reviews. However, Joe had no coding experience and limited funds to outsource the development process.

The No-Code MVP Solution

After discovering Glide Apps, a no-code app-building platform that allows users to create mobile applications using Google Sheets as a database, Joe decided to give it a try. He started by collating a list of local businesses, their contact information, and their products or services in a Google Sheet.

Using Glide Apps, Joe quickly transforming the data from the Sheet into a functional app prototype. He designed appealing user interfaces, added functionalities like filtering businesses by category or location, and implemented a user registration process to capture emails, introduce updates, and collect reviews.

The Validation Process

Joe shared the MVP of his local business directory with a small group of friends and acquaintances, requesting honest feedback on the app's usability, design, and overall concept. The feedback was overwhelmingly positive, with most users finding value in the ability to easily discover and contact small businesses in their area.

With concrete evidence of demand and interest, Joe decided to expand his app to other neighborhoods and, in the process, attracted offers of collaboration from local organizations and businesses who appreciated the visibility and support his platform provided.

Scaling the MVP

As Joe added more businesses to his directory and the user base grew, he continued refining the app and adding new features based on user feedback. Employing Glide Apps allowed for simple, real-time updates to the mobile app without requiring technical skills or complex processes.

Joe ultimately launched the full version of his Local Business Directory app, offering both a free version and a subscription-based model with additional features, such as push notifications and promotions. Using the initial success of his no-code MVP, Joe attracted investors and set the foundation for launching similar apps in other towns and cities.

Key Takeaways

Joe's experience demonstrates that no-code tools like Glide Apps enable aspiring entrepreneurs to rapidly create, test, and validate mobile app-based business ideas. Leveraging these platforms can help you:

- Build a functional MVP in a short period of time
- Test your idea with real users and gather meaningful feedback
- Iterate and refine your product without technical limitations or costly development processes
- Attract investors and collaborators with tangible success stories
- Scale your solution by tapping into a community of enthusiasts and partners who can help bring your startup idea to life

10. Case Studies: Real-World No-Code MVP Success Stories

There's no better way to learn about the potential of no-code MVPs than to dive into real-world success stories. These case studies demonstrate the power of no-code tools to bring innovative ideas to life quickly, efficiently, and without the need for technical expertise. Let's take a look at some of the most inspiring no-code MVP success stories from startups and entrepreneurs around the world.

10.1 Sharetribe: Online Marketplace Magic

Sharetribe is a perfect example of a no-code MVP that expanded into a full-blown product. Initially, it was conceived as a simple online marketplace for local sharing and trading – a concept that could be tested and validated with a no-code MVP.

The team behind Sharetribe used Bubble, a visual programming platform, to develop their MVP. They were able to create a powerful online marketplace in a matter of weeks by leveraging Bubble's user-friendly interface and features like responsive design, payment processing, and social media integration. The success of Sharetribe's MVP quickly validated their idea and attracted initial users and investors.

Since its humble no-code MVP beginnings, Sharetribe has grown into a fully-fledged online marketplace platform, catering to thousands of entrepreneurs and enabling the creation of diverse marketplaces without the need for custom code.

10.2. Outseta: Scaling Up with No-Code Tools

Outseta is a SaaS (software as a service) product that provides early-stage startups with an all-in-one solution for CRM, subscription billing, and marketing automation. The founders were aware of the urgent need to test and validate their idea in the highly competitive SaaS market.

The team turned to no-code tools like Zapier, Airtable, Carrd, and Typeform to create a seamless, fully-functioning MVP in record time. By using these tools, they could automate essential workflows, track user behavior, generate reports, and validate crucial product assumptions without spending resources on custom code.

The successful no-code MVP allowed them to iterate quickly, adapt to feedback, and ultimately scale their business to new heights. Now, Outseta enjoys a dedicated user base, a suite of powerful features, and a strong position in the marketplace.

10.3. Voiceflow: From Idea to Acquisition

Voiceflow, a platform for designing and building voice and chatbot applications, began as an idea to make voice design more accessible to non-developers. The founders decided to leverage no-code tools to build an MVP to test their product rapidly and attract early users.

The Voiceflow team utilized Adalo, a no-code app-builder, to create their MVP and get it up and running. Thanks to Adalo's user-friendly interface and customization capabilities, they built an MVP that provided an exceptional user experience and demonstrated the possibilities for voice design.

The no-code MVP caught the attention of investors, and the Voiceflow team eventually secured over $4 million in funding. Today, Voiceflow has thousands of active users, and the company has been acquired by ProtoPie – further proving the potential of no-code MVPs to fuel startup success.

10.4 Quotr: Streamlining the Sales Process

Quotr is a startup focused on simplifying the sales quoting process for small and medium-sized businesses. Instead of hiring developers and spending months building a product, the founders built an MVP using Webflow, an accessible and powerful no-code website development tool.

The Quotr team leveraged Webflow's functionality to create a fast, responsive, and visually appealing user interface that could effectively demonstrate the value of the quoting tool to potential customers. In just a few weeks, they had a fully functional MVP and began onboarding early users.

The no-code MVP allowed Quotr to rapidly validate its idea, quickly adapt to user feedback, and begin building its brand in the highly competitive sales technology space.

Lessons from Real-World Success Stories

No-code MVPs have allowed these startups to test and validate their ideas with minimal financial risk and limited resources. These examples demonstrate the possibilities that no-code tools can offer for entrepreneurs, validating ideas, iterating quickly, and ultimately, creating successful and scalable businesses. Entrepreneurs looking to follow in these startups' footsteps should consider embracing no-code tools and strategies to launch their MVP and kickstart their business journey.

10.1 No-Code MVP Success Story: Tara Reed's Apps Without Code

Background

Tara Reed is a Detroit-based entrepreneur who has successfully built and launched a number of profitable app-based businesses without writing a single line of code. She did this using the no-code MVP methodology and is now teaching other aspiring entrepreneurs her secrets of success through her platform, "Apps Without Code".

In this case study, we will take a deep dive into how Tara turned one of her unique ideas into a profitable business using no-code tools and methodologies.

The Idea: Kollecto

Tara came up with the idea for Kollecto, an affordable and personalized art advisory app, when she realized that she wanted to find and buy art for her home, but found the process of searching for and selecting art to be overwhelming.

She knew that there must be other people out there that faced the same problem, so she decided to create a solution that would provide access to art curators who could help find and recommend art pieces on a budget.

Building the No-Code MVP

To validate her startup idea, Tara first created a landing page using Strikingly which communicated the value proposition of Kollecto and included a simple "Get Started" call-to-action.

The landing page served to collect email addresses of interested users who were looking for a curated art-buying experience, allowing her to validate if there was indeed a demand for her business.

To further test her idea, Tara used Typeform to create a questionnaire that asked potential users about their art preferences, budget, and the level of personalization they wanted for their curated art suggestions.

Once she gathered enough responses, Tara outsourced the curation aspect to a group of art experts she found on freelance websites like Upwork. The art curators would analyze the responses submitted by users and then send personalized art recommendations via email.

Initially, the service was offered for free as Tara continued to iterate on the user experience and better understand the needs and preferences of her users.

Validating the Idea

As the number of users grew and the feedback became increasingly positive, Tara decided to monetize Kollecto by implementing a subscription model. By charging a monthly fee, she was now able to test whether users were willing to pay for the personalized art recommendations.

To implement the subscription model, Tara used a no-code tool called Zapier to connect her Typeform questionnaire with a payment processor such as Stripe, PayPal, or Square. This allowed her to collect payments without any manual intervention and scale her business more efficiently.

Kollecto continued to grow and Tara began to experiment with different pricing tiers to see which worked best to optimize revenue and customer satisfaction. Users were given the option to select a membership plan based on their art-buying needs, and Tara soon discovered the sweet spot in terms of pricing that maximized revenue while keeping the service accessible to a wide range of art enthusiasts.

Scaling the Business

The no-code MVP version of Kollecto was already achieving great success, but Tara wanted to take it to the next level.

To do this, she decided to build an actual Kollecto app that would provide users with a more seamless and visually appealing experience. Using no-code app development platforms such as Bubble and Thunkable, Tara was able to create a fully functional app tailored to her users' needs without the need to hire expensive software developers.

The app ultimately helped Kollecto grow even further and become the successful business it is today.

Lessons Learned

Through her experience with Kollecto, Tara Reed has proven the power of no-code MVP methodology. By starting small and using readily available no-code tools, Tara was able to validate her idea, test her assumptions, and scale her business without needing to write a single line of code.

Tara's success story serves as a prime example of what can be achieved when entrepreneurs embrace the no-code mindset and focus on customer needs rather than technical limitations.

As a result, Tara now teaches the no-code MVP methodology to aspiring entrepreneurs through her online platform, "Apps Without Code", allowing others to follow in her footsteps and quickly bring their own business ideas to life.

Case Study 1: Pipe: Building a Fintech Platform

Background Pipe is an innovative platform that allows companies to trade their recurring revenue streams on a marketplace. In simple terms, Pipe helps businesses get paid faster by transforming their SaaS subscriptions into up-front revenue. The platform is both beneficial for businesses looking for cash flow flexibility and investors seeking investment opportunities with fixed, recurring returns.

The Problem The founders of Pipe, Harry Hurst, Josh Mangel, and Zain Allarakhia, identified a significant need for businesses to gain greater control over their cash flows. Traditionally, this type of financial flexibility was only attainable by taking on debt or selling equity in the company. Both options come with drawbacks, such as potentially losing control of the business or being burdened by long-term debt.

The No-Code MVP To quickly test the concept without investing time and money in traditional development processes, Pipe's founding team turned to no-code tools. With no technical background, they needed a way to build a Minimum Viable Product (MVP) to validate their idea and attract initial customers.

Using tools including Bubble, Airtable, and Zapier, the team managed to build a fully functional MVP within just ten weeks. This allowed them to demonstrate the platform's capabilities to users, investors, and stakeholders without heavy financial or time investments.

These tools allowed the Pipe team to create and iterate their MVP, focusing on features such as:

- Secure authentication and user management
- Data input and management for revenue streams
- Trade execution and management
- Financial reporting and analytics

The Results With their no-code MVP, Pipe's team was able to validate their idea quickly and secure a user base that provides valuable feedback for the product's continuous improvement. As a result, they were also able to attract significant investments and partnerships.

In less than two years, Pipe has raised more than $66 million in funding and attracted major investors, including Shopify, Slack, and HubSpot. The firm's recent valuation exceeded the $2-billion mark, making it one of the most successful no-code success stories.

Lessons Learned

This exceptional success story showcases the power of no-code MVPs to bring innovative ideas to life rapidly. The key takeaways for aspiring entrepreneurs are:

1. **Speed:** Building an MVP quickly enables you to test your idea and iterate, reducing time to market and the risk of wasting resources on a product that may not have traction.
2. **Flexibility:** With no-code tools, you can remain agile and continuously adjust your product to meet user needs effectively.
3. **Reduced Risk:** Lower barriers to entry (fewer technical skills required and minimal upfront financial investment) mean you can test innovative ideas without putting your entire business at risk.

Case Study 2: Wild Audience: Revolutionizing Marketing Automation

Background Wild Audience is a marketing automation platform that helps businesses create personalized and automated customer journeys. Using behavioral tracking, the platform recommends relevant content and offers to each website visitor, resulting in better user experiences and increased conversions.

The Problem Bastian Ernst, the founder of Wild Audience, saw a need to improve the efficiency and effectiveness of content marketing. He believed that businesses should be able to deliver targeted content that truly resonated with website visitors, rather than relying solely on generic information and calls-to-action.

The No-Code MVP Just like Pipe, Wild Audience's MVP was built using no-code tools. Bastian first started with a simple version created with PipeDrive, offering a basic service to help businesses improve their marketing efforts. As he gathered feedback from initial customers, he slowly added features to the product.

To build a more sophisticated marketing solution MVP, Bastian used a combination of no-code tools, including:

- Typeform for creating interactive forms and capturing user responses
- Zapier for integrating and automating workflows between applications
- Google Sheets for storing customer data and tracking performance metrics
- ConvertKit for automating email marketing campaigns

The Results As the Wild Audience MVP gained traction, Bastian was able to secure a growing number of users and continuously gather feedback for enhancement. Wild Audience now serves clients worldwide, and its customers have reported impressive results, such as up to a 50% increase in customer revenue directly attributable to the platform.

Lessons Learned

Wild Audience's no-code MVP success story demonstrates the power of using simple yet powerful tools to test an idea in a cost-effective manner. Aspiring entrepreneurs can learn from the following key points:

1. **Iterative Development:** Through continuous feedback and improvement, you can keep users engaged and turn your MVP into a thriving, successful product.
2. **Integration:** The effective use of no-code tools can enable seamless data flow between applications and create a powerful, interconnected product.
3. **Lean Startup Mentality:** By focusing solely on the features that provide actual value to users, you can ensure efficiency and avoid wasting resources on unnecessary features.

As these case studies prove, a no-code MVP has the power to transform ideas into successful businesses. By utilizing the right tools and adopting a user-centric mindset, you can emulate this success and build a startup that truly resonates with your target audience.

Case Study #1: Sharetribe – Building Online Marketplaces

Sharetribe is a quintessential example of a successful no-code startup that allows users to create and launch their own online marketplaces without any coding skills. The platform is designed to streamline the process of building modern web applications that function as a marketplace for various kinds of businesses, such as renting, selling, and buying goods or services.

The Problem

Antti Virolainen and Juho Makkonen, the founders of Sharetribe, identified a problem many entrepreneurs faced: building and launching an online marketplace was a complex and daunting affair, often involving expensive investments in hiring developers or outsourcing the development process.

Many entrepreneurs with great ideas for online marketplaces were deterred by the costs and the technical expertise needed and, as a result, struggled to turn their ideas into a reality or validate their concepts before fully committing to development.

The Solution

With the vision to make the process of creating online marketplaces accessible and hassle-free for entrepreneurs, Sharetribe was born. The founders set out to build a platform that would simplify the process and allow users to create their own marketplaces without needing any coding skills. They used several no-code tools and put together an MVP to test their concept.

The No-Code Tools

To build the Sharetribe platform, Antti and Juho utilized some popular no-code tools, which helped save time and resources as well as kept the costs to a minimum. A few of these tools included:

1. **Bubble**: A visual web development platform that allows users to create fully functional web applications without writing any code. Bubble was used as the primary development framework to build Sharetribe's interface and backend.
2. **Zapier**: A tool that offers seamless API integration between different web applications without needing any coding. Zapier was utilized to connect Sharetribe's platform to external services like payment gateways, email automation tools, and social media platforms.
3. **Airtable**: A powerful spreadsheet and database management tool used for internal tasks such as managing customer data, content planning, and project management within the Sharetribe team.

The Results

Sharetribe quickly gained traction among entrepreneurs looking to create their own online marketplaces. By offering a cost-effective, easy-to-use solution that allowed users to build and launch marketplaces without significant technical expertise or investment, Sharetribe was able to validate its business model and turn the platform into a profitable business.

Today, Sharetribe powers thousands of online marketplaces around the world, helping entrepreneurs bring their ideas to life – all without writing a single line of code.

Key Takeaways

The story of Sharetribe showcases that the no-code movement isn't limited to only MVPs but can also power successful, full-fledged businesses. Using no-code tools, the founders of Sharetribe rapidly prototyped and validated their marketplace concept, proving that it's possible to change the way businesses operate and cater to their target audience.

For entrepreneurs aiming to build their startups using no-code tools, the key lessons from Sharetribe's success include:

1. Focus on identifying and understanding the problem you are trying to solve. In Sharetribe's case, the founders were well aware of the challenges entrepreneurs faced when launching an online marketplace, which allowed them to develop a platform that solved that problem with great accuracy.
2. Choose the right no-code tools that suit your needs and help you efficiently build the product you're envisioning. Don't be afraid to mix and match tools to create a tailored solution for your business.
3. Never underestimate the power of no-code tools. Many successful businesses have been built using no-code platforms, and embracing them can help save time, resources, and provide a solid foundation for the future growth of your business.

Copyrights and Content Disclaimers:

AI-Assisted Content Disclaimer:
The content of this book has been generated with the assistance of artificial intelligence (AI) language models like CHatGPT and Llama. While efforts have been made to ensure the accuracy and relevance of the information provided, the author and publisher make no warranties or guarantees regarding the completeness, reliability, or suitability of the content for any specific purpose. The AI-generated content may contain errors, inaccuracies, or outdated information, and readers should exercise caution and independently verify any information before relying on it. The author and publisher shall not be held responsible for any consequences arising from the use of or reliance on the AI-generated content in this book.

General Disclaimer:
We use content-generating tools for creating this book and source a large amount of the material from text-generation tools. We make financial material and data available through our Services. In order to do so we rely on a variety of sources to gather this information. We believe these to be reliable, credible, and accurate sources. However, there may be times when the information is incorrect.
WE MAKE NO CLAIMS OR REPRESENTATIONS AS TO THE ACCURACY, COMPLETENESS, OR TRUTH OF ANY MATERIAL CONTAINED ON OUR book. NOR WILL WE BE LIABLE FOR ANY ERRORS INACCURACIES OR OMISSIONS, AND SPECIFICALLY DISCLAIMS ANY IMPLIED WARRANTIES OR MERCHANTABILITY OR FITNESS FOR ANY PARTICULAR PURPOSE AND SHALL IN NO EVENT BE LIABLE FOR ANY LOSS OF PROFIT OR ANY OTHER COMMERCIAL OR PROPERTY DAMAGE, INCLUDING BUT NOT LIMITED TO SPECIAL, INCIDENTAL, CONSEQUENTIAL, OR OTHER DAMAGES; OR FOR

DELAYS IN THE CONTENT OR TRANSMISSION OF THE DATA ON OUR book, OR THAT THE BOOK WILL ALWAYS BE AVAILABLE.

In addition to the above, it is important to note that language models like ChatGPT are based on deep learning techniques and have been trained on vast amounts of text data to generate human-like text. This text data includes a variety of sources such as books, articles, websites, and much more. This training process allows the model to learn patterns and relationships within the text and generate outputs that are coherent and contextually appropriate.

Language models like ChatGPT can be used in a variety of applications, including but not limited to, customer service, content creation, and language translation. In customer service, for example, language models can be used to answer customer inquiries quickly and accurately, freeing up human agents to handle more complex tasks. In content creation, language models can be used to generate articles, summaries, and captions, saving time and effort for content creators. In language translation, language models can assist in translating text from one language to another with high accuracy, helping to break down language barriers.

It's important to keep in mind, however, that while language models have made great strides in generating human-like text, they are not perfect. There are still limitations to the model's understanding of the context and meaning of the text, and it may generate outputs that are incorrect or offensive. As such, it's important to use language models with caution and always verify the accuracy of the outputs generated by the model.

Financial Disclaimer

This book is dedicated to helping you understand the world of online investing, removing any fears you may have about getting started and helping you choose good investments. Our goal is to help you take control of your financial well-being by delivering a solid financial education and responsible investing strategies. However, the information contained on this book and in our services is for general information and educational purposes only. It is not intended as a substitute for legal, commercial and/or financial advice from a licensed professional. The business of online investing is a complicated matter that requires serious financial due diligence for each investment in order to be successful. You are strongly advised to seek the services of qualified, competent professionals prior to engaging in any investment that may impact you finances. This information is provided by this book, including how it was made, collectively referred to as the "Services."

Be Careful With Your Money. Only use strategies that you both understand the potential risks of and are comfortable taking. It is your responsibility to invest wisely and to safeguard your personal and financial information.

We believe we have a great community of investors looking to achieve and help each other achieve financial success through investing. Accordingly we encourage people to comment on our blog and possibly in the future our forum. Many people will contribute in this matter, however, there will be times when people provide misleading, deceptive or incorrect information, unintentionally or otherwise.

You should NEVER rely upon any information or opinions you read on this book, or any book that we may link to. The information you read here and in our services should be used as a launching point for your OWN RESEARCH into various companies and investing strategies so that you can make an informed decision about where and how to invest your money.

WE DO NOT GUARANTEE THE VERACITY, RELIABILITY OR COMPLETENESS OF ANY INFORMATION PROVIDED IN THE COMMENTS, FORUM OR OTHER PUBLIC AREAS OF THE book OR IN ANY HYPERLINK APPEARING ON OUR book.

Our Services are provided to help you to understand how to make good investment and personal financial decisions for yourself. You are solely responsible for the investment decisions you make. We will not be responsible for any errors or omissions on the book including in articles or postings, for hyperlinks embedded in messages, or for any results obtained from the use of such information. Nor, will we be liable for any loss or damage, including consequential damages, if any, caused by a reader's reliance on any information obtained through the use of our Services. Please do not use our book If you do not accept self-responsibility for your actions.

The U.S. Securities and Exchange Commission, (SEC), has published additional information on Cyberfraud to help you recognize and combat it effectively. You can also get additional help about online investment schemes and how to avoid them at the following books:http://www.sec.gov and http://www.finra.org, and http://www.nasaa.org these are each organizations set-up to help protect online investors.

If you choose ignore our advice and do not do independent research of the various industries, companies, and stocks, you intend to invest in and rely solely on information, "tips," or opinions found on our book – you agree that you have made a conscious, personal decision of your own free will and will not try to hold us responsible for the results thereof under any circumstance. The Services offered herein is not for the purpose of acting as your personal investment advisor. We do not know all the relevant facts about you and/or your individual needs, and we do not represent or claim that any of our Services are suitable for your needs. You should seek a registered investment advisor if you are looking for personalized advice.

Links to Other Sites. You will also be able to link to other books from time to time, through our Site. We do not have any control over the content or actions of the books we link to and will not be liable for anything that occurs in connection with the use of such books. The inclusion of any links, unless otherwise expressly stated, should not be seen as an endorsement or recommendation of that book or the views expressed therein. You, and only you, are responsible for doing your own due diligence on any book prior to doing any business with them.

Liability Disclaimers and Limitations: Under no circumstances, including but not limited to negligence, will we, nor our partners if any, or any of our affiliates, be held responsible or liable, directly or indirectly, for any loss or damage, whatsoever arising out of, or in connection with, the use of our Services, including without limitation, direct, indirect, consequential, unexpected, special, exemplary or other damages that may result, including but not limited to economic loss, injury, illness or death or any other type of loss or damage, or unexpected or adverse reactions to suggestions contained herein or otherwise caused or alleged to have been caused to you in connection with your use of any advice, goods or services you receive on the Site, regardless of the source, or any other book that you may have visited via links from our book, even if advised of the possibility of such damages.

Applicable law may not allow the limitation or exclusion of liability or incidental or consequential damages (including but not limited to lost data), so the above limitation or exclusion may not apply to you. However, in no event shall the total liability to you by us for all damages, losses, and causes of action (whether in contract, tort, or otherwise) exceed the amount paid by you to us, if any, for the use of our Services, if any. And by using our Site you expressly agree not to try to hold us liable for any consequences that result based on your use of our Services or the information provided therein, at any time, or for any reason, regardless of the circumstances.

Specific Results Disclaimer. We are dedicated to helping you take control of your financial well-being through education and investment. We provide strategies, opinions, resources and other Services that are specifically designed to cut through the noise and hype to help you make better personal finance and investment decisions. However, there is no way to guarantee any strategy or technique to be 100% effective, as results will vary by individual, and the effort and commitment they make toward achieving their goal. And, unfortunately we don't know you. Therefore, in using and/or purchasing our services you expressly agree that the results you receive from the use of those Services are solely up to you. In addition, you also expressly agree that all risks of use and any consequences of such use shall be borne exclusively by you. And that you will not to try to hold us liable at any time, or for any reason, regardless of the circumstances.

As stipulated by law, we can not and do not make any guarantees about your ability to achieve any particular results by using any Service purchased through our book. Nothing on this page, our book, or any of our services is a promise or guarantee of results, including that you will make any particular amount of money or, any money at all, you also understand, that all investments come with some risk and you may actually lose money while investing. Accordingly, any results stated on our book, in the form of testimonials, case studies or otherwise are illustrative of concepts only and should not be considered average results, or promises for actual or future performance.

tolerance, and the ability to consistently apply the strategies and techniques discussed.

Printed by Amazon Italia Logistica S.r.l.
Torrazza Piemonte (TO), Italy